To Begin Again

To Begin Again

A Life of Tragedies and Miracles

Virginia Jean Wesley

Library of Congress Control Number: 2009913651
ISBN: Hardcover   978-1-4500-1589-9
                  Softcover   978-1-4500-1588-2

To order additional copies of this book, contact:
Xlibris Corporation
1-888-795-4274
www.Xlibris.com
Orders@Xlibris.com
62328

For Page and Taylor and Griffin;

and in memory of my mother, my father and Sybil

Dedication

I am dedicating this book, my first published book, to Michael Paul Wesley. He was my first husband and my daughter's father. We were married for twenty-five years, and he was the first love of my life. I loved this man harder than I have ever loved anyone.

I want to thank him for his bravery and extraordinary courage in serving our country, the United States of America, during the Vietnam War. He was commissioned as a first lieutenant at the age of twenty and sent to serve as a platoon leader. He was wounded under hostile fire and returned home in March 1969. To the best of his knowledge, he was the only survivor. He was awarded a Purple Heart and Bronze Star with oak leaf clusters for his valor.

Michael represents a huge group of individuals, men and women, who remain unappreciated for their service in a war that the American people turned against. He turned against it as well, but it was too late. He did what he was trained to do and has paid a terrible price for serving in a war that was fruitless. Vietnam will always be a black scar on our Nation's history. May our government learn from its mistakes.

Michael survived against all odds. He was my first tragedy. He was my first miracle.

Acknowledgements

Thanking friends and family is in order; however, there is one person at the top of my list. My lifelong friend, Meggie Flaskamp, has been in my face for years about writing this book. She has always reassured me that my story was and is amazing and needed to be told. She is my muse and always makes me laugh at myself. I adore Meg.

Of course all of my friends are special, so I will begin by thanking everyone mentioned in the book because they all contributed to the tapestry of my life and this story. Special accolades to all the oncology nurses at Memorial Hospital and the Rocky Mountain Cancer Center; they are actually angels here on earth. I am grateful for my new oncologist, Dr. Timothy Murphy, because he is open to Eastern medicine, and I just like him as a person.

I want to extend special thanks to all of my Wise Woman friends who I like to refer to as goddesses.

Lynette Swann is my goddess of golden friendship that endures through the years and renews big time every time we see each other even if it's been a decade.

Jan Koch is the goddess of garden and design. She transformed my pathetic backyard into a Zen-like garden and temple for peaceful contemplation and playground for my grandchildren.

Melanie Salazar is the goddess of the Big Picture and artistic creator of my sunflower tattoo. She also introduced me to my totem animals.

Wendy Nelson, owner of Blue Fox Photography, is the goddess of visual beauty and photographed many of the pictures in this book and has immortalized my grandchildren.

Ruby Reid is the goddess of motherly love and my retail mentor because she always gave the best advice and was there for me at every turn.

Judy Permut is my goddess of beauty, intelligence, and patience. She is my protector and always knows when red flags are appearing.

Sharon Schulman is my goddess of herbs and healing, who knows when I should get up and leave.

I want to express gratitude to my new family at Cucuru Art Gallery and wine bar because they have energized me and fortified me out of true friendship. Thank you, Guillermo, and all the Alvarado brothers and Ellie for always saving me the best seat.

Grateful thanks to Karen London for our sisterhood in good times and bad and Linda Bofenkamp for showing me my printer was also a scanner.

Huge thanks to Denny Mahoney, my new business partner, in Happiness Heals for recognizing that this is my calling and the way we can help people and give back for all of our many blessings.

And finally to JD, thank you for making me gut laugh like no one else ever has and providing me with endless material for fantasizing.

I received invaluable assistance from Xlibris for providing me a stress-free method for publishing my book. I made the excellent new friends of Rose Alconga, my Submissions Assistant, and Marian Lumayag, my Copyediting Representative, Carolyn Gambito, my Design Consultant, Meagan Arevalo, my Publishing Consultant, and Riki Sayon, my Author Services Representative. It has been a pleasure working with professional yet personal people from start to finish.

I'm in lockdown at Memorial Hospital's emergency unit in Colorado Springs. I don't know that I'm in lockdown yet though. The ambulance arrived with a very handsome tall blond EMT guy at my side. I only agreed to go in the ambulance because he said he would ride with me while I lay in the bed in the ambulance. "Who's going to pay for this?" I ask. He says, "Unfortunately you will." I was just approved for Medicare June 1, but it has a $200 deductible. Oh, well. He promised we could talk all the way to the hospital. I really loved this arrangement because then I could stare at this beautiful young guy and I could tell him my story of two miracles in six months. First, I asked him if he had any children, and he said he had a ten-year-old daughter. I told him I owned Mountain Moppets, the children's store one block down the street on West Colorado Avenue. I sold it three years ago before the recession to someone who loves it as much as I did. He should take his daughter there because they have girls' clothing up to size 16, beautiful, quality clothing that is age appropriate and hip at the same time. Ten-year-old girls are already learning about fashion and being cool. He likes learning about the shop and *me*. I watch his eyes, and I know he can't really react to what he feels, so he just stays steady, and when we get to the hospital, he delivers me safe and sound to the guy that takes me on the stretcher into the new wing of the hospital. He says he likes my Uggs boots that I paid $23 for in China. Now a nurse tells me to pee in a cup, strip down to my panties, and put on two hospital gowns, one that closes in the front and one that closes in the back. This feels a little humiliating, but I keep my sense of humor and follow directions. The next step is the insurance information. Now that we're done with that, they put me in a sterile new room with a television. Oh good, Michael Jackson is on! I haven't seen much coverage because I got rid of my TV and made a little temple where it used to be. I would like to take this opportunity to say that I have always adored Michael Jackson, weirdness and all. No one will ever dance like that boy. He transformed the face of dance and music forever. I would always get so turned on when he would dance or sing. No matter what the song or video from *Dance with Me*, to the ultimate *Thriller*, he just had it all goin' on. You had to get up and dance. As Deepak Chopra said, "He gave a whole generation ecstasy when they danced to his music." He was a complete and total original from the white sequined glove to the white beaded socks that he loved so much.

They took away my purse with my glasses in it, but unbelievably, they let me keep my cell phone. My lifeline to my people. I know my people with a few exceptions. One of the first people I called was Lili, my son-in-law's mother. I was pissed off. When she answered the phone, I said, "Leigh, did you know that your son, Chas, called 911 and told them that I might be a danger to myself and possibly others? I'm at Memorial Hospital." She says she's coming right down to the hospital and that she loves me so much, which really pisses me off even more, and I want to say "drop the Christian thing for once," but instead I say, "Leigh, you have to take a stand. Chas has anger issues, and don't come to the hospital. I don't want to see you." I was driving Taylor to meet Griffin and him for lunch at Mountain Mama's. I was following him and at twenty-first and Colorado Avenue, I saw he was turning right, and I wanted to turn left so I could pick up a dress at Barracuda Bazaar. It's right on the way. We were stopped at the light, so I yelled at him that I was going to Barracuda, and he yells back at me, "Ginny, you go straight to Mountain Mama's." I say, "I'm going to Barracuda." What the hell! I'm his mother-in-law. Honor thy mother-in-law. So I turn left and go four blocks, turn right, and park behind Meadow Muffins. There is Chas right behind me. Taylor jumps out of the car and expects to go into the store with me. Taylor and I are best friends. She and Griffin are my reward for all the shit I have gone through in my life. So anyway, Chas parks next to me and has the phone to his ear and says in a very normal voice, "Taylor, come over here with daddy, and we'll wait for Gigi to come back and then we'll go to lunch." So I head into Barracuda, one of my favorite boutiques in Old Colorado City. I know the owner, Rebecca, who is especially cute, and her ex-husband, Eli, who is movie-star gorgeous. We spent a lot of years together on the avenue. I'm hurrying because I know Chas is waiting. I talk as fast as I can, which is really fast, to catch her up on all my miracles, and after she runs my credit card, I turn to leave. What happens next is still almost impossible for me to believe. Five very handsome men in gray uniforms were coming in the door and looking at me. What is going on? It crosses my mind that maybe they are going to sing "Happy Birthday" to me since my birthday is coming up. Did Dewayne arrange this? He has done amazing birthday things for me before. I'm mad at him though because he's on the fence about what Page is suggesting about me: that I'm manic.

One of the gorgeous guys says, "Are you Virginia Wesley?" "Yes, I am." "Your son-in-law called 911 and reported that you may be a danger to yourself and possibly others." "Oh, this is ridiculous. I know my daughter thinks I'm manic, but I've had two miracles in six months. Don't you think a person would be unusually happy because of that?" "Yes, I think you would." "So what's the problem then?" "Well, we'd like to take you down to Memorial to have you checked out by an emergency doc and a psychologist just to be safe." "I'm not willing to do that because my experience in emergency at Memorial is a ten-hour wait while my daughter is throwing up and suffering and we aren't seen because we are the least serious case there, even though I feel like she is dying." "Come on, Rebecca, help me on here." So Rebecca comes over and holds my hand and says, "Listen, I have a lot of mania and bipolar in my family, and Ginny Wesley is not the face of that. She is famous in this neighborhood. She owned Mountain Moppets for twenty-five years. We served on the merchant's association board together. We've known each other for years. Give her a break. She's had two miracles." Now the cutest EMT says, "Do you know a psychologist you could talk to?" "Well, yes, Kirsten Akse is right down the street. She helped me get through my daughter's robbery at gunpoint and the aftermath of her PTSD when she went into a cycle of multiple incidents of uncontrollable vomiting. I thought she was dying because she lost so much weight. We could go to her office, which is four blocks down the street, and knock on her door if she's there, but you have to schedule an appointment you know. This happened about ten years ago." Now all those boys disappear and have a powwow. It's been about an hour, and now Dewayne shows up. His bankruptcy practice is right above Mountain Moppets in the building we used to own together. He rents now because we sold the building before the recession, thank the universe. He is my second ex-husband. He's a prince and the most generous man I have ever known, but I'm pissed off at him because he's on the fence thinking I might be manic. So what? To me manic is extreme happiness. What do you want to do about it? Is there a limit on how happy you can be? After the powwow, the cute tall blond EMT comes over to me and says, "I don't see any way to move this thing forward other than to take you down to the hospital. Your family is worried about you." "Should I get my car?" "No, we'll just ride in the ambulance." "Who's gonna pay for that?" "I guess you will, sorry."

So it's one in the afternoon when I'm in my room watching Michael Jackson and have just hung up my cell phone with Leigh. Who else can I call, an ally? Meg. I have to leave a message. Jan. She is there, thank the universe. She is very specific in telling me to tone it down, just act very calm, and do what they say because this could quickly turn into an unwanted battle over my grandchildren. Point well taken. Who else? I called so many friends, I can't remember, but I definitely had all thumbs up for me after that. My best guyfriend, Mark Tierney, called me every day for a week after to make sure I knew he was there for me. We are very close for a lot of reasons. He is one of my symbols. He saved me when I was going through the biggest challenge in my life, when we didn't know if Page was going to live or die. She was two years old. He really did save me. We are very connected; we have always been. He is so special to me. He was in my first wedding as a groomsman. I had to correct him when he said usher. I think we will always be together. I'm not sure in what way. I know that I want to be with him as much as I can. He has two little girls: O'Neil and Mave also known as Fife. They are the same ages as my grandchildren. Mark is one year older than I am. We have been to Jamaica twice together, once to Negril and once to Port Antonio. More about that later.

I notice that Page is wandering around the desk area and then comes toward my room and actually enters. I can hardly look at her because I am so pissed off. I said, "Page, I told you I would see Kirsten Akse, and you were supposed to make an appointment for me, and you dropped the ball, as usual." "Well, I couldn't find her number, and I've been so stressed out because of you. Mom, we're all doing this out of love. We are all so worried about you." "Oh, that sounds like Leigh talking: 'We just love you so much.' That's her answer for everything that she can't handle." "You shouldn't be here, Page. I can't stand you right now. Get out of my room! You have a funny way of showing how much you love me, by having Chas call 911. This is ridiculous, Page. You can't possibly think I will benefit by being forced to see a psychologist. There is nothing wrong with me. Everything is right with me, Page. I am so happy and joyful, and you are trying to interfere with that, and I don't know why." "Mom, you're manic." "No, I am not! Get out of my room!" I yell out to the desk/nurses' station. "Get her out of my room!" She leaves and tries to argue with the nurse, but they tell her she can't come back in.

Finally at three thirty an ER doc comes in my room. I start talking really fast because I have so much to say, and he says, "Will you shut up a minute so I can talk?" "Well, okay." Then he starts to talk really fast, and I say, "You must be manic too, because you talk faster than I do!" He says, "Why do you think I'm an emergency room doctor?" and I say, "Well, why do you think I'm a writer? We have to have some place to put all that energy!" He says, "Touché! Pretty soon you are going to see the psychologist, and she's going to ask you a lot of stupid questions and then you'll be out of here, okay?" Oh, thank you, God, maybe I can still salvage my day because this isn't any fun. I'm determined to make my life all about fun. I'm really a fun girl; ask any of my friends. Yep, they will always say, "Ginny is so much fun!"

All of a sudden a guy a few rooms down starts yelling, "Help me, save me, Jesus, save me, Jesus" over and over again and louder and louder until some men come running and restrain him. It takes a while with quite a few men working together and then everything is quiet again. I go to the bathroom right across the hall and then I wander into the room next to mine. There's a young girl, maybe about twenty years old, and she's cute and sitting cross-legged on the bed. She has a tank top on and a bunch of tattoos. I say, "What are you in here for, honey?" "Depression." Then I say, "Well, guess what, I'm in here because I'm too happy!" "Do you want to trade?" she asks. "Yeah, how about if I take half of yours and you take half of mine and then we'll both be totally flat!" "Oh no, I'd rather be depressed than flat." "Well, I'd rather be happy than flat, so I guess we can't trade." "Get back in your room and sit on the bed!" says a person out in the hall. I realize he must be a guard because he had a uniform on and a gun in a holster. I just didn't notice him before because that picture is not part of my world. I say, "Am I in lockdown?" and he says," Yes, ma'am, you are. Now get in your room and sit on the bed!" "I will get in my room, but I don't feel like sitting on the bed. I'd rather dance!" I'm thinking this guy likes his job because he can try to control people. Not me, I can't be controlled. Ask Chas or Dewayne.

Now I start calling my people again. They took my purse and my glasses, but not my cell phone. I'm going a little nuts now, and I'm bored. I need more fortification and support from my troops. Somebody tells me it's been pouring rain outside for hours. There are no windows in the hospital/jail room, so I'm not aware of that. Oh no, the baby finches, Beep-Beep and Stella, have been outside all day! I had no idea I would be at the hospital all day. I'm keeping them at my house even though they were a present for my granddaughter, Taylor's, fifth birthday. She and her brother, Griffin, like to keep them at Gigi's house so they will be safe. I feel panicked, so I start calling people, and I finally get Lynda Dunne, my great friend who is always there for me when I need her. She says she'll go over to my place with her granddaughter and put the birds inside. It's getting late now, almost eight thirty. Shit, this is so ridiculous! Finally at nine a psychologist comes into the room and introduces herself. She tells me she's going to ask me some questions that might upset me, but it's part of her job and what she has to do when dealing with a patient like me. Whoa! I start to tell her my story about two miracles in six months, and she is taken aback. Nonetheless she continues with her questioning. She is way, way younger than I am, and so was the ER doctor. They are just babies compared to me in life experiences. So ridiculous! She asks me questions like, "Do you go to bars and pick up men indiscriminately?" "No." "Do you hear voices?" "No." "Do you think you have special powers?" "No." "Do you spend a lot of money on impulsive things?" "No." I had to think about that one in my head because I just got back from China a few weeks ago, and I did spend a lot of money there. I had to because who knows when I'll get back there. After all, I got freshwater pearls for US$17, Uggs boots for $23, and Ralph Lauren black label cashmere sweaters for $68 when they are listed in the online catalogue for $595.

She finally leaves, and I'm starting to feel really tired. I call Dewayne and ask him to come and pick me up because I think I will get out soon. The two doctors come back at eleven and say they don't believe I am a danger to myself or anyone else. They would like me to see a psychologist of my choice. Unfortunately, I picked Kirsten Akse.

I get dressed when they bring my clothes, and Dewayne shows up and drives me home. I am just exhausted. When I go into my house, I find Beep-Beep all alone in the destroyed birdcage. Stella is not in the cage, and Beep-Beep looks terrified in the corner. She must have gotten out when Lynda and her granddaughter tried to get the water-filled dishes out of the cage. I was so tired; I was having a hard time standing up. I managed to clean out the cage and put water and birdseed in there. I covered the cage with a towel and put on my jammies and fell into a deep, deep sleep until ten the next morning.

Now let's go back to the beginning. I swear I couldn't make a story like this up in my wildest, most creative and fanciful imagination, and I have a powerful imagination! What has happened to me in my life is really the most amazing saga of tragedies and miracles; I can't even believe it myself. So let us begin. I'm going to tell you all about it. I have a very keen memory and instant recall.

I was speaking to my sister-in-law, Patty, on a recent trip to Minneapolis, and I said, "Nothing in my life could have prepared me for what was to come." I was feeling a little melancholy but happy at the same time. She replied, "You *were* prepared because your mother loved you unconditionally." That hit me like a ton of bricks because I knew that was a true statement. So that started me thinking. Life does begin with your relationship with your mother. I was born on August 11, 1949, the youngest of three and the only girl, which was most fortuitous for me. My brothers were five and ten years old respectively. My mom was almost forty when I was born, so as you might imagine and as she told me many times in my life, "When you were born, honey, my doctor exclaimed, 'Helen, you hit the jackpot!'" She would tell me, "When the nurses brought you to me for the first time, you had little pink bows tied into your hair all over your head because you had so much thick dark hair." From the day I was born my mother thought I was the most beautiful baby she had ever seen and never wavered until my own daughter, Page, was born. When she studied her face, she said she really didn't look like me; she looked like her father, but she was a glamorous baby because she had curly copper-colored hair and long curled black eyelashes and brown eyes. She was thrilled we named her Page because that was her maiden name. At that time my elder brothers did not have children, so again she thought she hit the jackpot because she was finally a grandmother. What I know now and she knew then is that having grandchildren is the best that life has to offer. It's your reward for all the shit you've been through in your life.

Ginny at 5

Matt and Ginny and Tom

I met Page's father when I was fourteen years old. I had just returned from two weeks at summer camp in northern Minnesota with a few of my best friends. I soon found out that another group of my friends had been doing something very different while I was away. They were meeting boys from another part of town, mostly Catholic boys from private schools. These girls let me know that they had picked the ones they liked the most, but that there was one guy left who was really cute and they saved him for me. I remember being curious and kind of excited to see whom he might be. It wasn't long before I met him. My first impression was that he was tall enough for me because I'm 5'10" and he was 6'2". Perfect! My next impression was that he was big. His feet were a size 13, he carried just a little extra weight, and he was clumsy. He had dark red hair, brown eyes, and a beautifully sculpted nose. I thought he was very handsome. I decided right away I wanted to know more about him, and I think there was the beginning of a small sexual attraction, but I'm not sure of that now. I figured out right away that he was really smart, smarter than I was for sure. The story of his young life started to unfold, and I learned that it was very different from mine. First of all he was the eldest of eight kids. *The Minneapolis Star and Tribune* featured a story on his neighborhood, which revealed that there were fifty-two kids living on the one block where Michael's family lived. There were four more kids to arrive in his family, two cousins and two more babies before his mom was finally finished having children. That summer we met we hung out together when we could, mostly with the group because most of us didn't have our driver's licenses yet. I remember that one of the guys, Mark Somers, had a Vespa, and we would take turns getting around on that. Today they are back in fashion and available in an array of designer colors. I would love to have a green one now. We were so cool. I was disappointed to learn that Mike was going back to a private boarding school run by Jesuits in Prairie du Chien, Wisconsin, at the end of the summer. Why was he going there? What I came to learn was a story of abuse and violence that my young mind could never have imagined.

Mike's father was a very successful entrepreneur who owned a packaging plant not far from their home. I'm sure the pressures of supporting eight children and employing dozens of people created a lot of stress in his life. His method of coping was self-medicating with alcohol. He had that nasty hereditary gene for alcohol addiction. Both his mother and father, as well as many of his uncles, were alcoholics. He ran his company in a very professional manner and treated his employees with the utmost respect. All of his employees loved him and worked hard for him. The way he ran his family was an entirely different matter. Terror reigned in the Wesley household.

Mike's mother was a lovely woman who was totally overwhelmed with her life of raising eight children and coping with an alcoholic husband. Her home had four bathrooms and there was a dirty diaper in every toilet most of the time. She did have a cleaning lady who worked three days a week. She would begin each week cleaning the basement, and the second day she would clean the main level, and the third day she would clean the upstairs. I think Mary really was in love with Dick, but after all the children and alcoholism, she was balancing on a dangerously precarious tightrope.

Dick had a pattern of coming home from work, and depending on how his day went, some kind of drama ensued. Mary and the children lived in a constant state of anxiety and fear because they never knew what his arrival would bring. I think he had a certain amount of constraint with Mary, but Michael, being the oldest child, was the next in line as the recipient of his wrath and rage. I now believe that there was some kind of gene present in some of the Wesley males that was responsible for their excessive rage.

Michael hated his father when I met him. He learned that I was an extremely sympathetic listener because of my emotional nature, and I was beginning to fall in love with this tortured young man. I too started to hate his father because I couldn't understand how a father could treat his son so badly. According to Mike's younger sister, Patty, one day Mary was insisting that Mike mow the lawn. She probably pestered him until the teenager made the huge mistake of calling her a bitch. Being incensed and hurt, she lost no time in calling Dick at the office to tell him what had happened. Michael began the task of mowing the lawn finally and could not hear what Mary and all the kids who were hanging around heard, which was the screeching of tires in the driveway about five minutes later. Dick got out of the car and marched around to the backyard, punched Mike in the head with a closed fist, and knocked him out. He left him lying on the ground, marched back to his car, and went back to work. Mike never even saw his dad. I soon became aware that this type of violence was not uncommon when Dick was around. It happened enough that Mary devised a plan to get Mike away from his father for the whole next school year. She told me later that she was really afraid that Dick might kill him. The school of choice was Campion. It required testing and admission standards. Mike had been tested earlier for his IQ, which turned out to be in the genius range. That might have been his ticket in. He boarded a train at the end of the summer and went off to the Jesuits. As they say, absence makes the heart grow fonder, and our love affair really began then with letters back and forth in his junior year. That was my sophomore year in high school, and it ended my interest in any other boys in my school. I really yearned for this beautiful young man. He was a little dark, but very sensitive, and made me feel special. I also felt like I was his emotional lifeline. He would tell me about all of the antics of his friends at this all-boys school and the slightly weird behavior of the Jesuits, like paddling of bare ass in the cellar of the sanctuary. Mike's roommate was George Wendt, the actor. The anticipation grew as Thanksgiving and Christmas vacations approached. I was seriously in love by the time he arrived back from all those months away. I couldn't wait to see him. I thought about him constantly, and the more I learned about him, the more I loved him. He always had intelligent, irreverent things to say. I just thought he was the most handsome and wonderful thing that had ever happened to me. I felt that way for many years to come.

Another wonderful thing was happening at the same time I was falling in love with Michael. I was getting to know his sister, Patty. She was five months younger than I was and went to a private Catholic girls' school in town. We were both 5'10", and she had very long blonde hair and a beautiful face. I liked her immediately and realized that she had many of the same issues with her father that Mike did, but there were problems with her mother as well. She was the eldest daughter, and so much was expected of her. I couldn't believe what her life was like. My mom hardly asked anything of me except maybe make my bed and put my dishes in the dishwasher. There was a family that I came to know starting in second grade that had three sisters—Annie, Jillie, and Meggie, and I just adored them. Their mom was also a very cool woman, and I loved her too. I eventually started to call her B. They used to invite me over on Saturdays or Sundays to rake leaves or do other chores because they thought I needed to learn how to work, and then their dad, Mr. Flash, would take us out for ice-cream sodas at the local drugstore fountain counter. He was also a very cool man. He was a prominent criminal defense attorney and trial lawyer, but I didn't know that at the time. I knew he was gone a lot, but when he was home, he was fun to be around. I love those memories. We all loved each other.

Patty's memories start at about age eight. Her mother told her it was her turn to change her brother Jimmy's diaper. She went to his crib upstairs and found him with a gross dirty diaper, and he had smeared his own feces all over the walls and the crib. How does an eight year old process that sight? Somehow she managed to clean him up and the walls and the crib and report back to her mother. It seemed to her that her mother lay on the sofa in the family room a lot. I think she must have experienced major depression. More memories involve coming home from school and being told to change out of her school uniform and into her playclothes so she could begin her chores. She would be instructed to rinse out all the dirty diapers that were soaking in all four bathrooms in the house. The worst part was that the littler kids would pee or poop on top of the diapers because there was no other choice for them. So then Patty would have to reach her hand down in the toilet to get the diaper, flush the toilet, and then rinse the diaper. She felt like Cinderella. Next she would dash around the house hanging up clothes and jackets, always filled with anxiety and fear that her father would be coming home from work soon. She was always thinking about damage control. I didn't always work. Dick arrived home one day and came in the house, but Patty didn't see or hear him come in. She was having a discussion with her mom, who had just said something mean and derogatory to her. Patty was hurt and responded accordingly. Just then Dick walked into the room and heard that part of the conversation. He grabbed Patty by her blonde hair, pulled her to the floor, and proceeded to kick her and hit her with his fists, spewing out venomous words until he was finished. Another time the whole family was sitting at the dinner table, and there was one more person at the table. It was the new baby sister, Julie, who was seated in a high chair, and Patty was feeding her. The next child in line after Michael and Patty was Joanne, and she was explaining about a speaker who was at their school that day. He was a black man who was lecturing on something or other. Immediately Patty could sense that Dick was becoming agitated, and she tensed up with fear. Then Dick looked at Patty and said, "If you ever bring home your nigger boyfriend, I'll kill him and then I'll kill you." Patty protested and said she didn't have a black boyfriend. Dick got up from the table and left the room, and Patty realized he was drunk. A little while later he came back into the kitchen and came down on the top of her head with two closed fists with all his might, grabbed that blonde hair, pulled her off the chair, and punched and kicked her in front of the entire family, including her mother. He left the room, and nothing was said. Patty said Michael wasn't there because he would never have let that happen because he was bigger than his dad at that point. Michael was still at Campion for his senior year, but he was kicked out permanently for some disciplinary issue. His grades were excellent. He came back on the train with all his belongings. I was so happy. I knew he would be in trouble with his parents, but I would get to see him all the time, which was so exciting. He enrolled in the public high school in their district just one suburb over from mine. I was in heaven. Now I could go to all the school dances such as homecoming and prom with him. His parents loved me and treated me like a special new daughter. They were way nicer to me than to any of their own kids. I sort of got in the inner circle and consequently witnessed a lot of things I would rather not have known about.

My mother fell in love with Michael right along with me. She thought he was so smart and handsome and a really good conversationalist unlike her own two sons, who were selfish and self-absorbed.

Both of my brothers were born on October 13 on a Friday exactly five years apart. They seem like polar opposites to me, but I think in reality they are both very much alike. My eldest brother was very mean to his little brother and very resentful because the baby dethroned him from his position as the only child for five years. The middle child, Matt, was sweet and sometimes sickly and so cute with curly blond hair. There were tales of many injuries to Matt because Tom would push him or put him in harm's way. One story my mom told me was how Tom and his best friend took Matt on a toboggan ride down a steep hill with lots of trees dotting the landscape. They were heading straight for a big tree, so the two friends jumped off and left the five-year-old little brother to crash into a tree. He ended up with multiple stitches in his head.

My eldest brother was indifferent to Mike, but my brother Matt was pretty nice to him. Mostly Matt was interested in my girlfriends. Mike spent quite a lot of time at my house because life was so miserable at his house. He took refuge at my house one night after his dad punched him out again. His mom was pregnant with his sister, Julie, and she just freaked out; he left and came over to my house and said he wasn't coming back. He'd had it with his dad, just couldn't take it anymore, all the verbal and physical abuses were breaking him down. My mom was ready to call the police; she could not understand how a mother would not protect her son. My mother was an emotionally strong woman and very protective of all of her children. She didn't take criticism of her children lightly. At that point she was pretty disgusted with what I would tell her was going on over at the Wesleys. Mary called our house for Mike, and I handed him the phone. She begged and pleaded for him to come back saying that she might lose the baby because she was so stressed out. I think he spent the night in our basement and then went back home the next day.

Julie was born in March, and she weighed 13½ lb. Mike and I had conspired to skip school that day. We did, and we both were caught. My mom was a pushover about it, but Mike got in a lot of trouble and was grounded for a while. I had my driver's license by then, so we could still see each other if I went over to his house. That was fun because I could see Patty also, and no matter what Mike had to do around the house for his punishment, I was happy just to be near him. I started being asked over to his house for dinner every Sunday night. I loved it in the beginning, but started to dread it a little bit toward the end. The Wesley house was really where I learned to work. I had some odd jobs in high school against my mom's protests. She didn't want me to do any manual labor. Mike's mom would always cook the Sunday meal, and it would always be really delicious. She was cooking for nine children now, two cousins who had been taken away from their alcoholic mother and now lived with the Wesleys, me, Dick, and her. She used every pot and pan that she had in her kitchen and then we would all sit down at one ginormous table with two overflows at the counter. Every kid had milk from a five-gallon milk machine that was across the room by the refrigerator. Everyone could have as much milk as they wanted and oftentimes would have the best roast beef and meats that money could buy. Dick was never cheap. He was making a lot of money by this time, and Mary could spend whatever she wanted on groceries. The deal was that Mary cooked the dinner and all of the kids were supposed to clean up. I thought that was very fair because she had all those kids plus the cousins and cooked the entire dinner. Usually it was very nice unless someone spilled his or her milk. That would infuriate Dick, and he really couldn't lose his temper or hit anyone if I was there, so I wasn't an eyewitness to any real violence. After dessert, everyone was excused, and Mary and Dick and all the boys, including Mike, left the kitchen never to be seen again. The other older girls except Patty and me and Maggie, the cousin, would somehow disappear to go to the bathroom or whatever excuse they could think of and never return. So there we were, the three of us, to clean up the entire kitchen, including mopping the floor, which Patty did and sometimes Michael would come back to do. It literally took hours to clean up that kitchen with all three of us working hard and nonstop. I remember being physically exhausted by the end and wanting to go home to my quiet bedroom. I was usually too tired to do much homework when I got home. Looking back though, those are very precious memories for me because I really came to love Patty like a sister that I never had.

I loved having Mike home because we got to go to all the dances together at both of our high schools. His parents really liked me and started including me in all the family activities. Then sometime after Mike's graduation from high school, during the summer another bad thing happened with his father. There was always a lot of verbal abuse like "You're never going to amount to anything. You're an idiot."—all that abuse when he knew Mike was way above average intelligence and even at the genius level. Why? I'll never understand why he was so mean to this wonderful son of his. Actually now he was a man and way bigger and stronger than his father. For whatever reason Dick walked into Mike's room and just punched him out. I could never understand why Mike didn't defend himself. I thought he should just deck his dad to make him stop, but he never would. So that was about the last time Mike ever lived at home.

He was able to move in with a friend, Tom Fulton, who ran in our crowd and whose parents went to Europe for the summer with their youngest daughter and left their downtown apartment with the two guys. They had owned a house on Lake Minnetonka outside of the twin cities, and it was completely destroyed in a tornado the previous summer. It seemed strange that they replaced this wonderful home on the lake with a high-rise apartment in downtown Minneapolis. Maybe they were ready for a change of lifestyle. That seemed a little extreme to me. We used to have some great parties at the boathouse that survived the tornado. It had just enough room to get a keg of beer in. I became really good friends with all of the guys that hung around with this crowd. Some of us are still good friends today. That's when I acquired the nickname "Legs" in reference to my long leggy body. That summer was so much fun. I have many fond memories of the innocent antics of the bunch of us teenagers. There was quite a lot of drinking and smoking, cigarettes only. Pot hadn't hit the Minneapolis scene yet, but it wasn't too long until it did. After all, it was 1966 and the revolution was right around the corner.

Mike worked all summer at a job that only required manual labor, and he was anxious to start his college career at the University of Minnesota. I remember that he quickly became bored with his classes and was not sure what his major should be even though he was interested in history.

The war in Vietnam was the big focus of our generation at that time. The draft was in place, and all of our friends were worried about where their number would fall in the lineup. This was serious anxiety for everyone, brothers and sisters, sons and daughters, mothers and fathers. The war was escalating, and it was a relief that Mike was in college and had a student deferment. Then he did something that totally rocked my world. He and a good friend, Bill Bofenkamp, went down to the draft board and enlisted together in the army. I remember I was scared about what was going to happen, but he was sure he wanted to go and fight for our freedom. He was idealistic about fighting communism and being an American soldier. It was hard to argue with that, and I became very defensive of his position even as the antiwar sentiment was growing among college students.

I was looking at being without him during my senior year in high school and that seemed like a real bummer because I knew I wouldn't have dates for homecoming or my senior prom. I was really sad that we would be apart, but I was never one to miss out on any fun, so I made the best of a hard situation by keeping in close contact with all of my many friends. I was usually included in everyone's plans. Having as much fun as possible was very important to me. I always had an extremely sunny outlook on life.

I knew everyone loved me, and I loved him or her right back. Except for the sadness and yearning I was to experience while Mike was away, I think I experienced euphoria almost all of the time. I was in love with my life for as long as I could remember.

When Mike's parents learned he had enlisted in the army, they did a really cool thing. They both planned a going away party for him and invited all of our friends. The theme was a pig roast with all the trimmings in a sort of nightclub setting. They brought in a lot of little round tables with tablecloths and candles on each one. Each table seated four, and there were about six or eight of them. I thought it was just magical, and the food was phenomenal, all made right there in the kitchen by the two of them. Who would have dreamed that would happen? Patty was a server; of course, she wasn't included as a guest because she was Mike's younger sister. It didn't matter because by then she knew I loved her, and Mike was starting to take her seriously as his ally. After all, they both knew all the ugly secrets of the Wesley household and had experienced them together.

With Mike's impending departure, I know I was fretting and worried, but I was busy modeling as a teen board representative for an upscale department store Dayton's in Minneapolis and planning my future in college. I was in a small competition with my best friend, Jill, who was getting a lot of attention in our high school. She had been on the high-kicking line dancing team and was now captain of the team. She was nominated for homecoming queen. I actually had tried out for cheerleading, but had no talent in that department. I knew I was a good skier and a pretty good golfer at an early age, but I really didn't have the coordination for cheerleading. I also lacked the school spirit to even care. The love of my life was going off to war, and I thought it was more fun to be a model. I applied for the position on the teen board, and so did my well-honored friend. I was awarded the position, and my self-esteem was well intact by then. I had a blast doing the teen board thing, which included a professionally choreographed fashion show featuring the Yardbirds, who were a very popular English band at the time. I wore some of the most outrageous fashions in the show because I was tall and thin and kind of twiggylike. It was the late 1960s and that was the height of fashion at that time—big eyes, false eyelashes, long legs, and a flat chest. I definitely had all those things going for me. Jill had all those things too, except the flat chest. I think I also had something called moxie, which made the difference of me being chosen instead of her. The next item that dominated my life was where I was going to college. The University of Colorado at Boulder was the only choice for me. A few years earlier Helen and Harold (my mom and dad), my brother Matt, and I took a road trip to deliver him to junior college in Durango, Colorado. I was fourteen years old, and this was my first visit to the state of Colorado. It was also the first time I experienced the feeling that my heart was going to jump out of my body. The visual beauty of the entire state of Colorado, in my opinion, is unsurpassed by any place in the world that I have seen.

Granted, I haven't seen the entire world, and many places that I have seen are exquisitely beautiful, but something about Colorado spoke to my soul, and I have chosen to live here for all of my life, and have no intention of ever leaving. I applied for admission to only one school. I just knew I would be accepted, so when I received my letter of acceptance after waiting for the mailman every day for weeks, I was ready to get busy preparing for my flight from the nest. Some days when I waited for the mailman, he would bring me letters from Mike in whatever stage of training he was in. He was in training for a long time. First he went to boot camp in Washington State for six weeks. He wrote me how physically tough it was, and when he came home from basic training, he was transformed from a slightly overweight teenage boy to a totally fit, slim young man with a shaved head. I missed his thick auburn hair and learned that a bald head can be kind of bumpy. I was so happy to see him, but I knew it wasn't for long. He had been tested in basic training and found to be material for Officer Candidate School. An intelligent guy like Michael was singled out of all those thousands of new soldiers and slated for way more advanced training. He potentially had leadership skills, and leaders were needed in this war against an uncommon enemy. It was a ground war against an enemy so insidious that our troops could not even recognize who the enemy was most of the time. Men, women, children—anyone could be the enemy. It was also a war that was being fought in a jungle unlike anything we knew in this country. These people we were waging war against were small in stature and burrowed underground in expansive tunnel networks. Our soldiers were totally unprepared for this kind of an enemy.

So I went off to college and sorority rush week, and Mike went off to Officer Candidate School in Ft. Benning, Georgia. We were living in totally opposite worlds, but we stayed very connected by the written word and occasional phone calls. I received scores of letters from Mike, at least one or two a week, and I would always reply right away. We both loved to write, and our letters to each other were really what would be called love letters. I saved every one of mine, and now my daughter has them. I don't know if she's read them all, but if she ever does, she will know that we really loved each other from the beginning. Romantic love is very powerful and can last many years. That love lasted over thirty years for me.

Senior Year in high school

College was everything I dreamed it would be. I had a deal with my mom. She had inherited some money from her mom, so she let me go to CU, but only for two years because she could only deal with $8,000 expenditure. My parents did not save money for college or any other purpose because they just spent what they had coming in month to month. They ran with a very wealthy crowd of fun-loving people. There were always lots of parties and laughing. My parents knew how to have fun, and they managed to keep up with their friends' lifestyle because they had several inheritances and generous gifts from their parents. My dad was a charter member at the Country Club in our neighborhood because his dad bought him one of the first memberships. All of us kids benefited from that membership because we got to hang out at the pool all summer and charge hamburgers, malts, cokes, and french fries to my dad's account. He played golf and gambled with his friends every weekend. My mom was extremely happy with this arrangement. She just loved my dad, and as long as he wasn't gambling all the money away, she was very content. My dad never made more than $25,000 a year, but they just rubbed up next to people with money, and it was as good as the real thing. My dad was not a risk taker, yet all three of his children grew up to be entrepreneurs and owned their own businesses. My mom told me the story of how my dad was invited to be a partner in a friend's business, but he could

31

not make himself take the risk. He had three children, and he had a job with a large corporation and that was security. The friend made millions on the new business, and my dad was left behind. I don't think my dad ever recovered from that one.

My parents never discussed what was expected of me in college. I don't think anything was expected except that I would get married and my husband would take care of me. It didn't happen exactly that way. It seemed as though I was getting everything I wanted in my life. First I was chosen as the representative from my high school for that teen board and modeling position. Next I was accepted to the University of Colorado without even applying to another school. I just wasn't interested in any other one, not even the University of Minnesota, which would have been a slam dunk for me. My grades were good and my SATs were okay, but getting into CU was a gamble. I took the risk as I did many other times in my life, and it paid off. Now it was time for sorority rush week, and after all the parties, you were given a piece of paper to put your three choices on. I was very excited that I was given my first choice. I don't think I was that surprised. I also had the boyfriend I wanted; the only problem was that he was eventually headed to Vietnam.

Michael as 1st Lieutenant

At this point Mike was well into Officer Candidate School; in fact, I had a trip planned to visit him in Georgia for his eighteenth week completion of training party, which was a formal dance and dinner. He bought me the ticket so I didn't have to tell my parents I was going, since I would be flying out of Stapleton International Airport in Denver.

Before I went on that trip, I needed to make it through my first semester of college. Everything was going great for me as usual, and then disaster hit. I started having a very sore throat and swelling in my neck. I ended up at the infirmary with a diagnosis of mononucleosis. I had no idea how serious that would turn out to be. Somehow I convinced my parents that I didn't need to come home, and I tried to handle this nasty illness by myself. It was very tough to just make it through a day. I had an unrelenting cough, and I was so tired, I could hardly get up every day. I couldn't make it to class, so I had to figure out what to do as a new freshman about studying and grades. Just as I convinced my parents, I convinced all my teachers that I could do my work outside of class and just take my finals after Christmas vacation. I'm pretty sure I became slightly addicted to codeine cough medicine, which I was prescribed so I could catch a little sleep at night. That semester took a toll on me. When I finally made it home for Christmas, my mother almost fainted when she saw me. I had lost 16 lb, down from my already slim 5'10" frame of 128 lb. Now I was a gaunt 112 lb, which was totally in fashion at the time. Twiggy was the most popular fashion model of the time and precursor to the superskinny supermodels that are the rage today. Mike came home for a few days of leave and for some reason he thought I looked great. My eyes looked enormous on my thin face, and my legs were long and skinny. We all had a lot of fun over the holidays. Mike and I were a solid couple and deeply in love, but I was very young to feel that strongly about someone. All of my friends and family loved Mike too. I think there was a growing fear in all of us that he would be going off to war on the other side of the world, and a lot of boys were dying over there. The statistics were becoming shocking, and of course, the war was being televised. I believe that was the start of viewers becoming numb to the horrors of war. It was the beginning of excessively violent content in television programming. It was a revolutionary time in more ways than we would ever know. I was right smack in the middle of one the most amazing, wonderful, and powerful times of change in modern history. First and foremost there was the Vietnam War, which turned out to be a deep black scar on American history just like the Vietnam Memorial Wall in Washington DC depicts, with fifty-eight thousand names of dead engraved in black marble. Page and I visited the site when she was sixteen. We sat on a bench together staring at the wall, and I wept for a long, long time. I remember I could hardly compose myself enough to get up and walk the length of it and place my hand on the various panels along the way. A whole generation of young men and women were injured and died for no good reason in the Vietnam War. Mike was among one of the three hundred thousand injured. He was one of the lucky ones.

I spent the last week of my vacation studying for all my finals and happily went back to my exciting life at CU. I started hanging out with some very funny and good-looking characters the last half of my freshman year. I found myself to be an amateur matchmaker, always trying to put people together, never allowing myself to become interested in anyone because I was in love with a boy in the United States Army who would be going off to Vietnam eventually. However, there was one boy I became interested in. His name was David, and I allowed myself to be slightly intimate with him. It was fun, but I really only considered him a friend. He knew about Mike, but he fell in love with me anyway, and when I told him after Christmas that I couldn't see him anymore because Mike was coming to visit me on leave, he cried. I felt terrible, so I only had boys for friends after that and only allowed one other boy to kiss me or touch me in my whole experience in College at CU. He was very attracted to me, but he ended up being a jerk. I totally missed the sexual revolution of the sixties and seventies. It took me a long time to realize that practice makes perfect in lovemaking. I really imposed abstinence on myself. I was a virgin the first time Mike and I ever made love. I remember him being very sweet and gentle, and I don't know how experienced he was; I never asked. It didn't matter because I knew he loved me and I loved him. He was my dream come true and I hung on every word he said because I knew he was wise and intelligent beyond his years.

When Mike came to visit, I introduced all my new friends and sorority sisters to him, and everyone immediately liked each other, and most of us have remained friends for life. I've lost track of a few, but I've stayed in touch with the most special ones. Those long-lasting friendships surprise you sometimes when you least expect it, and the memories you have attached to them are priceless and, sometimes, hilariously funny. One that comes to mind is a bunch of us piling in one of my best friend's, Jill's, yellow mustang convertible, which she shared with her sister Annie, who went to school in Arizona. We weren't quite so spoiled back then, with most of us not even having a car in college. We were heading up to Aspen for a weekend of skiing, and the weather was quickly deteriorating. There was basically no visibility, and my friend, Jill, was letting my favorite guyfriend, Dean, drive. He was so funny and sarcastic; I just loved hanging out with him. He was like a best friend, only a guy. We seriously might have all been killed because the windshield quickly became a solid sheet of ice. Jill proved herself to be quite adept at reaching out of the side window with her arm and gloveless hand and catching the wiper as it swung back and forth in its usual rhythm, pulling off as much of the ice as she could. How scary to think we did things like that and didn't even think twice. That's the beauty of life. Many times it is worth taking risks when you are young because life can be so thrilling when you aren't afraid. I have come to realize that life is a total crapshoot most of the time. I feel lucky that I seem to have had good intuition with the really important decisions in my life.

There was a time during Mike's OCS training when he came to the realization that he really needed to try to get out of going to Vietnam. His roommate told him how he might be able to get an appointment to West Point. Somehow he was able to get an appointment from the senator from Minnesota Gene McCarthy. He made a trip to New York, visited the campus, and spoke to someone about signing on, only to learn that he would still have to go to Vietnam and then be committed to seven years of service after his education. That plan was not going to work, so he gave up the appointment.

The next step for Mike after graduating from Officer Candidate School and being promoted to first lieutenant was jungle training in Panama. As I was soon to learn, that meant he was going to survival school with a bunch of other officers to see who could complete the mission successfully. From what I know, they all set out into the jungle with a helmet, some matches, and their army-issued pack. There was no food, but they did have a rifle and a knife and the clothes on their back. The terminology the military used for this training was Escape and Evasion. To Mike it was a joke. Now he was starting to lose patience. He felt the whole training was contrived, and he was sick of the way everything was designed to be understood by the least gifted individuals.

Apparently he slept on trees because being on the ground in the Panamanian jungle at night was too dangerous. He cooked a snake in boiling water in his helmet and shot a tree sloth, which turned out to be covered with bugs and not edible. He made it back when everyone else quit. That set the stage for him learning that he was an expert at survival. He has remained a survivalist for all of his life. I have personally witnessed this many times.

He found himself on a military flight to Vietnam, knowing that he would be the leader of a platoon at age twenty. I can't imagine the enormity of that responsibility, but he had to accept it; there was no other choice. From the moment he set foot on the ground in Vietnam, he knew it was the biggest mistake he had made thus far in his life.

Paralleling his life was mine, living in a sorority house with a bunch of fun, beautiful, motivated, and mostly entitled girls. I was the only one who had a boyfriend in Vietnam. Mike's parents came up with a great idea for the two of us to keep in touch. They gave us both a tape recorder so that we could send tapes back and forth and really hear each other's voices. I remember being so excited when I would receive one of those tapes in the mail. He would talk to me from the top of an armored personnel carrier, which was really a tank with a machine gun on top. He was the gunner. There would be several guys inside the tank driving. I could hear all the popping sounds of guns firing in the distance, and he would be describing what was happening while they were moving along. Sometimes he would yell out to his men. I remember feeling so impressed and proud of my soldier man. On the other hand, I was sending him tapes of my life in the sorority house and life on campus. My friends would send him their best wishes, and of course, I would tell him how much I loved and missed him, and I really meant it. It was so strange living and experiencing two such different realities. I felt guilty.

Even though I was having a normal college experience, going to my classes and having fun with my friends, I was nervous about what was going on in Vietnam and the escalation of the war. There was more antiwar sentiment being spoken, and I found myself defending the war, but I was really defending Mike and the fact that he was putting his life on the line, and people were criticizing the soldiers themselves. My roommate was my childhood friend from Minneapolis, Jill, and she had a boyfriend from high school who went to Stanford. I thought he was arrogant and controlling, and I never thought he was so great as she did. He was very critical of the war and the soldiers who were fighting the war, and after a conversation or two with him and defending Mike's position, I just couldn't stand him. He ended up breaking up with my friend in a very cruel way. She flew out to San Francisco to visit him, and while she was there he introduced her to his new girlfriend, who happened to be Susan Haldeman, the daughter of the famous Haldeman who was part of the Watergate scandal.

I was so naive; I didn't expect the long-distance phone call from Mary Wesley when it came. I was in my room in the sorority house, having a conversation with my roommate, Jill, when the phone rang. I picked it up and there was Mary's voice on the line. Shear panic is what I felt at that one life-changing moment in time. She never called me at school. I knew something was wrong. She started babbling on about just getting home from a trip in the Bahamas and blah, blah, blah. "Mary, why are you calling me? Is it about Mike?" I heard the phone drop on her end, and I collapsed on the floor. In a few seconds Dick got on the phone and started telling me the bad news. Mike had been shot and was in a hospital in Japan. All I could think of was, "Please don't let it be a head injury!" I learned that he had been shot in his shoulder and flown in a helicopter to safety. Of course, there was a much bigger story, but I wouldn't hear it for a while.

Thank God, I wasn't alone, and Mike didn't die. I knew we would be together again, so I just waited for the next call. It came on the pay phone on the third floor of the sorority house. I just happened to be there in the middle of the day, and I heard that phone ringing way off in the distance. "Oh god, I better run up those three flights of stairs. It might be him." It rang and rang until I got there, and it was Mike, calling from Japan. How he ever got that phone number, I'll never know, but his voice was warm and soothing, and I was relieved and happy and so excited that I had proof that he was okay. He explained a lot of things to me about how he was going to get home with this injury in his arm. The doctors had to figure out what to do with his arm because a rocket that hit his tank had shattered the ball inside the socket of his shoulder. There was a lot of shrapnel embedded in his skin, and his wrist had been damaged as well. He would be coming home in a full body cast from the waist up with his arm sticking out to the side at a right angle, also in a cast, which was attached to the body cast. It was quite a contraption when I finally saw it. The trip home was not a pretty picture.

Vets coming home from Vietnam were not welcomed home or honored like they are today. It's one of the things I'm most ashamed of in our history. It still breaks my heart and makes me angry at the way the Vietnam veterans were treated when they returned home from the battleground. Mike's flight home was on a converted civilian airplane. It was converted into a makeshift flying hospital with flight attendants subbing as nurses and caregivers. I didn't know when his flight was coming, so I wasn't there when it landed, nor was anyone else. Apparently, it sat out on the runway for several hours before anyone was ever unloaded. No one was there to welcome them home or cheer for their bravery, just a long wait until someone came to unload them. Mike somehow managed to be placed at Fitzsimmons Military Hospital in Denver so he would be close to me, only thirty miles away in Boulder. He should have gone to Great Lakes Naval Hospital in the Midwest because that was closest to his hometown, but he was able to pull some strings because of his rank. I didn't have any wheels, but I sure figured out how to get some. I asked a sorority sister, Mary Smiley, if I could borrow her car to drive the half hour to Fitzsimmons Hospital. The reason she even had a car was because she had won a national beauty pageant. I think it was a brand-new Firebird, and I had to be really brave to ask way more than once to borrow it. Mary was tall and beautiful and had won the Miss Wool of America title. She won not only the car but also a $10,000 wardrobe from the wool manufacturers and a bunch of free travel to promote the industry. She was very kind to me because I'm sure she was breaking all the rules by letting me drive her car. I pleaded my case, and who could say no to why I needed it?

Driving to Denver the first time to see Mike was exhilarating, but very scary. I didn't know what to expect and wasn't prepared for what I saw. No one could have known what to expect with the number of injured far surpassing anyone's wildest imagination. They say medical technology advanced exponentially because of the types of injuries coming out of Vietnam. In previous wars the injured would not have survived the trip out, but thanks to the heroics of well-trained helicopter pilots, some amazing rescues were made. Some of the guys probably wished they hadn't been saved.

When I entered the hospital, I could see I would have to navigate the halls by myself. There was no extra staff anywhere, and I knew I needed to get up a floor or two. Greeting me when I stepped out of the elevator were hallways lined on both sides with beds filled with guys about my age in various states of misery. I think I tried not to look too closely and kept my focus on finding Michael. I finally found him in a sunny room with lots of windows, and there he was in his awkward-looking body cast all tan and handsome and happy to be back. I didn't know he would have lost so much weight. It turned out that everyone suffered from dysentery and diarrhea in Vietnam—one of the occupational hazards, so to speak. Mike's injury caused him a lot of pain and suffering. The rocket that hit his tank and sent shrapnel into his bone essentially exploded the ball inside the socket of his left shoulder. When it eventually healed, it didn't fit very well inside the socket and limited his range of motion. Also a major nerve was damaged in his chest, so there was quite a bit of atrophy in the arm, which was unavoidable. After the wound had healed enough, physical therapy began. The arm was never right again and was the source of pain from that point on. I learned about many weird injuries when I started to meet some of Mike's buddies in the hospital, really weird. One of his friends had caught a lot of shrapnel in the stomach, and all of his internal organs fell out of his body; he saved himself by putting the whole mess back in with his hands and held it there until the medics came. They had to sew his penis back on, and he could only have an erection that went down instead of up. Another guy lost a large part of his skull, and he had to live with a large metal plate in his head. When these friends found time to hang out, it was as if a bunch of misfits were drawn to each other because of their injuries. They tried to have a few laughs and smoked pot and drank massive amounts of alcohol to escape the horror of what had happened to their bodies and minds. I tried to hang in there with them, but it wasn't a good time for me. I wanted to get Mike away from their shenanigans because it was a time of more self-destruction.

Mike's job at the hospital while he was in rehab was not a bad one. He advised the injured vets on what their options were as far as being discharged. A few were offered the option of being medically retired with a lifetime pension and maybe some options for education, but the vast majority were given an honorable discharge and severance pay that amounted to about $2,000. Mike himself fell in the first category. It turned out to be the reason we could be married as soon as he was discharged. We could live on what he was given if he got right back into school because then we would have a living allowance as well as his tuition paid for plus the pension. He was classified with a 40 percent disability, which was the magic number to be considered for the retirement pension. The rest was completely arbitrary, I think. It must have made a difference that he was awarded the Purple Heart and Bronze Star with clusters. Only about eight hundred soldiers received the deal that Mike got. Then the system changed because it was too costly for our government.

So the wedding was planned. My mom went into high gear and planned everything the way she thought it should be. I got to choose my dress and the bridesmaid dresses, which was all I really cared about. My maid of honor was Annie Salmon, and the bridesmaids were Jill, Mary Harmon, a sorority sister, and Patty, Mike's sister. They were all tall and beautiful. I also chose the date so that all my friends would be home from college for Christmas vacation.

When I actually told my parents that Mike had asked me to marry him, my mom was not surprised at all, but my dad stood looking out the window in our den and cried. That's when I learned how sentimental my dad was. I think they were both a little worried that I was so young, but both knew that there was no point in bringing up any objections. They knew this was the real thing, and I would be twenty in August.

I loved my wedding except for the half hour on my knees in the High Mass ceremony in the Catholic church of my mom's choice. There was another problem too; it was on the Saturday of the Super Bowl play-offs that our very own Minnesota Vikings were vying for the title. Needless to say, there was a shortage of men at the wedding ceremony, but they all showed up at the reception for food and libations. My mom was in her glory, and I felt beautiful and special and very happy. I think Mike was happy too, but he looked a little pale. His pants were too short, and I learned the reason later when he told me what happened the night before at his parents' home, where all the relatives were staying.

Dick Wesley went all out for this wedding. Both Dick and Mary came from large Catholic families, so he tried to get as many brothers and sisters there as possible. They hosted a groom's dinner with sixty guests, and I'm sure it cost more than the whole wedding because of all the alcohol consumed. Apparently the aftermath at the Wesley home was a scene that was screen worthy. Dick's brother was so intoxicated after the dinner that he provoked a fistfight with Dick, and their mother was yelling and screaming at the two of them, she being intoxicated as well. Mike had to intervene and pull the two apart. They were all a bunch of drunks as it turns out most of the Wesley men were. After the fight, things finally calmed down, and every one made their way to the bedrooms. There was no bed for Mike because the relatives had taken over his room. He must have slept on the floor or a couch, which explained why he looked a little pale and tired at the ceremony.

I remember leaving the reception with everyone's good wishes and heading off in our new yellow MGB convertible that Mike bought with some sort of car allowance from the army when he was discharged. That car made no sense for us as a couple; it was tiny, and we were big people, but it was fun for a while. It was December 27, and we were headed up to Indianhead Ski Resort in the upper peninsula of Michigan.

41

The first five years of our marriage went well. The highlight was our trip to Europe. I put it all together after a plan to go to Guadalajara, Mexico, for art classes fell through. We had about $1,200 saved from a summer job Mike had with the city of Minneapolis on a road crew. He made about $6 an hour, which was a lot of money back then in 1972. We were able to get round-trip tickets for $169 on Icelandic Airlines from New York to Luxembourg. We drove our VW station wagon to New York with our really great friend Greg Duffy. We were all pumped about this adventure. We planned to go for three months. If we ran out of money, Mike's dad would wire us his retirement check, which was about $450 a month at that time. We had everyone's blessings because going to Europe at that time was really in vogue. Europe on $5 a day a piece. This was a true adventure—everything spontaneous, no plans, and no reservations. It may have been the coolest thing I have ever done. To do it with Mike was truly magical for both of us.

Can you imagine getting up in the morning and saying, "Where should we go today? Amsterdam, Paris, Florence, Geneva, Rome, Naples, Athens, Nice, Malaga, Barcelona, Morocco, Madrid, Munich, Garmisch-Partenkirchen." We went to all of those places and more. First we went to Amsterdam. Surprised? That's where the weed was. Menus of all the best high-grade pot in the world. Michael and Greg were on cloud nine. I just tagged along with those boys. They were on a mission—to stay stoned all of the time. I couldn't really keep up with them, but I sure had fun trying. I always have fun when the opportunity is there. I have certain memories that stand out. For example, I remember we went to The Paradisio and The Cosmos Fantasio in Amsterdam where all the student travelers from all over the world hung out. The common denominator was *marijuana*. It was 1972; the year Billy Davis was put in a Turkish prison. They made a movie about his experience called *The Midnight Express*. I was nervous when we were in Morocco mostly because Mike just seemed to have no fear as far as buying weed was concerned, which was definitely a no-no when we were in Morocco. I remember we boarded a bus in Spanish Morocco to cross over to French Morocco and we were kicked off in the middle of the desert. Mike's hair was too long and hippielike. We were standing alone wondering what to do, when a VW bus was just crossing out of French Morocco and we were able to catch a ride with them. Off in the distance I saw a caravan of people and camels.

We weren't about to give up. We had befriended an Arab kid before we got on the bus, and there he was when we got back to the original place. He helped us find a place to buy scissors, and I proceeded to cut Mike's hair. Short enough? Hope so. We got back on the bus with the Arab kid. He said he would ride to the checkpoint with us to make sure we got through. We put a paper bill of whatever currency we had, equal to about one American dollar, because that's what the kid said to do. When we stopped at the checkpoint, the guys with guns got on the bus. I was a little scared, but Mike and the kid made me feel less vulnerable. The kid took our passports and went up to the guard. No problem, we were through, and the kid gave us our passports back, waved, and got off the bus. A little cashola usually works, eh?

I remember Greg was not with us at that point. We must have split up way earlier. He definitely was not with us in Spain, which was later in the trip. He actually left us after two weeks when we arrived in Garmisch, Germany, an unbelievably picturesque town in Bavaria beneath the famous Zugspitz mountain peak. We stayed at the military base in guest quarters and dined on hamburgers and french fries and chocolate malts. It was heaven to be reminded of home in a friendly clean environment, and it was cheap to stay there—one of the many benefits of being medically retired from the U.S. Army.

Many travelers we met along the way told us not to bother with Paris because the French hated Americans. Mike stated his position on that emphatically. We were not going to miss the most beautiful city in the world because we listened to someone's biased opinion. He was always right and besides he spoke French well enough to get us by. We loved Paris. It was the most beautiful city architecturally. We took a day trip on the bus to Versailles. We were amazed at the opulence in the palace and wandered around the grounds of incredible gardens and statuary. I remember a pigeon pooping on my hair as it flew over. Funny which memories stick with you! We stayed on the west bank of the Seine where all the artists hang. Every day we went to a crepe stand by our hotel and bought my favorite treat for $1—a chocolate-filled crepe served in a cone shape filled with a whipped creme that was addictive. I had to have a second one later in the day. Two equaled $2 a day, which was a lot when we were trying to get by on $5 a day, but I just had to have it. By the time we hit the Louvre, I was totally burned out on museums, so we just sat on a bench and stared at Venus di Milo's *Ass*.

I kept a journal on our trip, but somehow over the years and because of the many moves, it is missing. My memories are endless, and I am able to recall so much that I can join in almost any conversation about Europe and tell an interesting story. I've been told many times that I have great stories. Our plane tickets had a return date, so we knew our trip was quickly coming to an end. We sat waiting for our flight back to New York, being grateful that we took this opportunity when we were young and carefree.

Crested Butte

After we returned from Europe I decided I needed a real job that brought a real income. I learned that the airlines were now hiring married women. Northwest Orient Airlines was the obvious choice since they were based in Minneapolis. Coincidentally one of my best friend's dad was the CEO. Donald Nyrop was the force behind Northwest's tremendous success during his most reputable career. Northwest was one of the only airlines that operated in the black for decades. When he retired, the airline fell apart. Many years of bad leadership and greed almost brought it down.

I never told him I was interviewing. I was hired on the spot. It didn't hurt that I was 5'10". The DC-10 and the 747 aircraft had just been purchased by most of the big airlines, and it was a real advantage to be tall because the overhead bins were so high. I started training almost immediately, and in six weeks I was in the air making a great salary with all the benefits and free passes for my family and myself. Michael was not happy about me being hired. I did have to be away three to four days a week, but I could arrange to have longer stretches of days off with creative scheduling. I liked flying at first, but I soon learned the routine with the pilots, and I didn't really like that. The crew would board the plane about half an hour before the passengers and that would give the pilots a chance to check out the flight attendants. They forgot about their marriage licenses at the gate.

I was married, so I made it clear that I did not appreciate their advances. I usually got along with all the girls and didn't mind sharing hotel rooms. If the crew had dinner together as a group, I would always join in the fun. I had never made that much money, so it was great to contribute more than ever before, and it empowered me to make decisions for myself. I established my own checking account and bought a brand-new bright yellow Volkswagen bug with a black racing strip. I qualified for the loan all by myself. I think Michael was miffed by my newfound independence. He didn't like me being away for days at a time. I should have paid more attention to his complaints. I didn't worry about him when I was away on trips. I trusted him; I knew he loved me. I didn't understand how unhappy he was. We didn't know about PTSD then.

One day I returned home from a three- or four-day trip and let myself into the apartment. I started unpacking and opened the closet in our bedroom. Utter shock and disbelief! All of Mike's clothing was gone. Everything! What was going on? I could not imagine what had happened. He must have called me then. "Mike, where are you?" "Ginny, I have done something you will never forgive me for." "What do you mean? Are you having an affair with Debby Martin?" It all flashed in front of me. He was attending classes at the University of Minnesota and would often give her a ride to class. She was my friend, but I wasn't that fond of her. She wasn't even pretty, and she sure wasn't very smart. Why her? "It's over, Ginny, it meant nothing to me."

We separated for the next eleven months. I still loved Mike, but I wasn't sure if I wanted to forgive him. Everyone knew about it. No one told me, and I was pissed off. I felt Mike needed to get away from the whole scene of his family and the drama of what had happened. His family and many of our friends were very disappointed in him. I was his sister's best friend, and she had a hard time understanding how he could possibly do that to me. Fortunately his best friend, Jim Crowley, had moved to Colorado and was staying in touch. He wanted Mike to move out and ski for the winter. Our life was about to take a beautiful turn because the ski town he was living in was Crested Butte. Michael left on a hiatus from our marriage during that summer.

I continued with my job as a stewardess and decided now would be the time to meet a few more men and test the waters. I actually had a brief affair with an unmarried pilot who ended up hurting me unintentionally because he was involved with another girl who had his child. The child had serious heart problems, and his attention naturally went to that. Sometime in the late summer I took a trip on a pass to Boulder to visit my friend Jill. She had graduated from CU and was working as a counselor in the dorms. It was fun to be back, and I was excited to see the old gang. We were invited to a party and that's when I met Noble.

He was a year older than me and was still in school trying to figure out what he should do with his life. The minute I met him I felt a vibration, a sexual vibration. He looked like an Adonis. His hair was a beautiful curly blond bleached from the sun to almost towhead. He was tan and healthy and a few inches shorter than I was. He was slightly withdrawn and quiet but that didn't stop him from making a big play for me. I was definitely interested in the gorgeous twenty-six-year-old boy. We found ourselves alone sitting on the floor talking for a few hours later in the evening. Everyone had gone home, and I told Jill I would get a ride to her place later. I ended up in a twin bed with him, and we had a very intimate sexual encounter. I wasn't sure I wanted to be that intimate, but he asked me if he could experiment a little because he had never been with a girl and had oral sex. I finally said yes because I enjoy that type of pleasure. That type of intimacy does tend to change the whole game.

Noble on the left Jill and boyfriend.

We spent the rest of my time in Boulder together. As I was getting ready to leave, he told me he was going to visit me in Minneapolis in a couple of weeks after my next scheduled flight with Northwest. His parents lived in Des Moines, and he was going there before school started up in the fall semester. He drove to my apartment from Iowa and spent four days with me. We joined some friends of Mike's and mine at their lake cabin for a weekend in northern Wisconsin. It felt so good to be adored again. I had great chemistry with Noble. I loved being with him. On the drive home in my new yellow Volkswagen bug I told Noble while he was driving that I was falling for him. "Ginny, you need to go back to Mike. He really loves you. You're the kind of girl who needs to be deeply loved, and I can't do that right now. I have problems." I knew that meant he had emotional problems, maybe depression, and I started to protest. "You can't fix it. I don't even want you to try." That was it. I never saw him again or even heard about him for thirty-five years. He did give me one more incredible night of sensuality though. We were sitting on the sofa in my apartment together listening to music on the stereo. We were drinking wine, and he positioned himself behind me and started whispering in my ear. It was something about what beautiful bone structure I had and then I just felt myself melting in his arms. We moved to the bedroom and became one for the last time. He was gone in the morning.

I joined Michael in Crested Butte not long after that. He had spent a lot of time amid nature there renewing himself, and when he told me he had changed, I believed him. I sold my Volkswagen bug for $500 more than I paid for it, bought a jeep, and headed out for Crested Butte, Colorado. When I arrived at my destination, it was love at first sight. Crested Butte, to me, is one of the most beautiful spots on the planet. The town itself sits at nine thousand feet and occupies a valley that is surrounded by a panoramic view of several mountain ranges all the way around. The crowning glory is Crested Butte Mountain itself with the crest rising up one side and then peaking to the side at the summit. A butte is a mountain that stands alone. It is the wildflower capital of Colorado. The recreation it has to offer is endless and exquisite. Mike and I lost no time enjoying all that Crested Butte is—a spectacularly beautiful product of nature that we were incredibly fortunate to enjoy for eleven years.

Our daughter was born there, and we bought our first home in that amazing place. We quickly accumulated a menagerie of wonderful interesting friends from all walks of life. The average intelligence in Crested Butte seemed to be higher than usual. There were quite a few trust-funders there, people who could choose where they wanted to live. We were fortunate that we had Mike's pension to fall back on if we didn't make enough money during the off-season. I felt like I was at camp, a very expensive luxury camp where everyone loved each other and would do anything to help you through rough times.

Page

I got pregnant two weeks after I stopped taking my birth control pills. It had been six years since Mike and I were married, and we were both thrilled and excited about having a baby. I had a dream pregnancy. I don't remember having morning sickness or any other problems associated with pregnancy. I only gained 25 lb and felt great right up until the day she was born. I did take a tumble down the stairs of our apartment and landed on my tailbone, so that was uncomfortable for a few weeks, but the pain subsided fairly quickly. I sat on a rubber donut and tried not to complain. I was too happy to complain. Mike and a group of our best friends planned a hiking and fishing overnight trip up to Twin Lakes, which was about a four- or five-hour hike. I wanted to go, but I was six months pregnant and I didn't think I should go. I pouted and felt left out until Michael convinced me to go, by assuring me that he would carry all the gear; all I needed to carry was a light daypack with water and a few candy bars. It was a beautiful day, and we got an early start. I could go at my own pace, and he would always make sure I was okay even if he hiked faster and was ahead of me. I felt great the whole way and enjoyed the incredible beauty of the trail through a magical pine forest and then opening up at the end to the steeper climb up to the lake.

I finally made it to the cheers and encouragement of our friends, Jackie and John, and another couple we love, Eric and Kathleen. Mike spread out a blanket for me to sit on and set me up with a fishing rod and reel. He put a worm on the hook and cast the first time and handed me the rod. He no sooner got his own fishing rod out, than I had a big trout on my line. He ran back to me and quickly took the beautiful rainbow-colored fish off the hook and rewormed it so I could cast again. Again I had a big beautiful trout on the line before he could cast his own reel. That happened ten more times until I had caught enough fish for everyone's dinner. I don't think Mike ever caught a fish that afternoon, and John maybe caught one. Nothing like fresh Rocky Mountain trout right out of the lake into the frying pan. We were a team, but I obviously was the winner!

Page was born on November 7 with no complications. I arrived at the Gunnison Hospital with Mike about three thirty in the afternoon and she was born at five. I dilated from two to ten in about fifteen minutes. My doctor, Jay Wolkov, didn't have time to put scrubs on. He delivered her in his street clothes. It was a totally natural childbirth, and our baby girl was perfect and unusually beautiful. The placenta broke into a million pieces, so Jay had his arm buried in my uterus for an hour. Mike got to hold her the entire time. He was in love with our little baby girl, Page. She had all ten fingers and toes, a red cast to her little bald head, and impossibly long and thick black eyelashes. She was a stunning baby.

We called my parents in Southern California when I was admitted to the hospital, and they left for Crested Butte within an hour to make the eighteen-hour drive. She was their first grandchild, so they were running on adrenaline. They were waiting at our newly purchased house when I came home from the hospital thirty-four hours later with my 5 lb 13 oz baby girl. My mom, Helen, took over from there. I hardly got to hold my baby girl for the next week. I let her do it because I knew she wouldn't see her again for many months. That Christmas we rented our house for $1,200 because we needed the extra money. I went to Minneapolis to introduce her to all the Wesley clan. Mike had to stay and be the property manager. The house needed to be supervised because it had a coal-burning furnace. My parents thought we were a little crazy for buying a one-hundred-year-old house, but I loved it. It was the first house we ever owned. We had moved fifteen times in eleven years. I was happy to own a house finally. We burned eleven tons of coal that year. It was the original mine doctor's house. We were told he performed surgeries on the kitchen table. Every day the clinkers had to be cleaned out of the furnace. When I came back, all my plants were dead, and the house was trashed. We never did that again.

Mike and I got used to being told by everyone that Page was the most beautiful baby they had ever seen. We got used to it, but never tired of it. When she was four years old, Bobby Brazell, our friend the photographer, took a picture of her, which he used for years to advertise his business.

When Page was about ten months, she started vomiting at least once a day for no reason. We started with Jay Wolkov, and he sent us to a specialist in Montrose who put tubes in her ears to no avail and that lead us to Minneapolis and then the Mayo Clinic. Something was very wrong, and I knew it, but I walked out on our appointment at the Mayo Clinic because my gut told me to. The head pediatrician put his big finger down her tiny little throat trying to make her throw up. "Why did you do that?" I asked feeling choked up and about to cry. "Because I want to see what she looks like when she vomits." I took her away from him and walked out with Nancy, Mike's sister, who accompanied me there from Minneapolis. Every one was mad at me, including Mike and his dad, who had pulled some strings to get us in. I chose to take her to Children's Hospital in Minneapolis instead with a referral from Dr. Mitch Enzig. He was a specialist in children's gastroenterology from Wayzata. Bettyann Flaskamp, my second mother, was behind me and supporting me all the way through what turned out to be the biggest challenge of my life. Keeping my baby alive became my mission in life for the next year.

After several surgeries, including a mastoidectomy and a Nissen fundoplication, it was determined that she had an unexplained growth in her ear. I remember the ear, nose, and throat surgeon coming out of the operating room to talk to me. Bettyann was waiting with me throughout the entire four-hour surgery. I noticed he had tears running down his face as he told me he had to clean all of the little bones in her inner ear, taking them apart. He couldn't determine where the matter was coming from, but it had filled her entire inner ear. They had biopsied the sample and determined it was normal cell matter from the ear. He ordered a CAT scan and advised us to try to be strong for the baby. Page's second birthday was in a few weeks.

We met with a neurosurgeon at the Children's Hospital two days later. Mike was there with me and so were both his parents, who were separated at the time. I couldn't comprehend what he was showing us on the films and telling us was her prognosis. There was a tumor in her inner ear lying next to her brain. It was about the size of a cigarette pack. It was a neurofibroma that was growing slowly and was inoperable because of its location. Oh my god, he said *inoperable*! Then that heartless man told me it would have been better if the tumor was malignant because at least they could try radiation. We all left feeling totally hopeless. I remember sitting in a rocking chair feeling completely numb and not being able to cry. I always cried at the drop of a pin. I was sick and depressed. They had cut up my beautiful baby, and now they were telling me she was going to die. Just as I felt myself sinking into the depths of despair, the surgeon who had operated on Page appeared. "I know what the neurologist told you, that the tumor is inoperable. I don't agree. Listen, I went to school with someone who was specializing in the type of surgery that Page needs. It's microscopic surgery like a dentist would perform. I need some time to find him. Take her back to Crested Butte and try to put some weight on her. I will call you there when I find him." That's all I needed to hear. There was hope. I knew I could handle anything now. There was hope.

We went back home to Crested Butte and waited. The call came. We had an appointment with Dr. Jack Pulec in Los Angeles in early February 1978. I'll never forget him or that day. My parents drove up from San Diego to be with us. We waited in his office for five hours after our scheduled time. He was a very sought-after and busy man. When we finally met him, I knew he was the one. He was the miracle worker. I adored him right away. "I've reviewed all of Page's films, and I can do this surgery and remove the tumor with the help of a neurosurgeon. We will do the surgery together. She is so young. Because of her age she has tremendous recuperative powers. She has a much better chance of full recovery than an older patient. She will be the youngest patient I've ever had. Let's get this surgery scheduled." I loved that handsome, brilliant man. He saved my baby. I will never, ever forget him.

Page's recovery was not an easy one. The surgery took eleven hours. They called three different times from the operating room to tell us Page was doing well. When I finally saw her, bandages were wrapped around her head with some cute little curls sticking out on one side. She was beautiful. They had warned us before we saw her that she had to have a tracheotomy and it would be temporary, but they didn't know how long. Her facial nerve was involved in the tumor, but Dr. Pulec was able to graft it with a nerve he took from her shoulder. They had to tie off her carotid artery, and if she didn't have a stroke in twenty-four hours, she would be normal. Her little body would reroute the blood on its own. She didn't have a stroke, but she did get pseudomonas meningitis. They had her on heavy antibiotics within minutes, so she pulled through fairly quickly. After the surgery she weighed 14 lb.

Page and I stayed in West Hollywood at Children's Hospital for the next two and a half months. I slept across the street at a seedy little hotel because it was so close. There was no Ronald MacDonald House back then. I would call the front desk so they could watch for me when I crossed the street late at night in the dark after a long day at the hospital. The Wesley girls took turns visiting me so I wouldn't be so alone. As usual I would try to grab some fun out of the experience, even though it was sobering for the girls to see how seriously ill Page was. She had a long way to go before she was ready to go home. When Mike's sister Joanne was visiting, we were invited to a roller-skating birthday party for Cher. Yes that Cher. There was a little boy in the hospital who was a burn patient. He had pulled a hot coffeemaker down on himself. I became friends with his mom. She invited Joanne and me to the party. Her husband was the conductor of Mac Davis's band. We had a blast strapping on the roller skates and wowing everyone because we were so tall. With skates I was 6' and Joanne was 6'4". Cher was an excellent roller skater and performed in the middle of the rink. Chastity was there as a little girl, and I remember meeting Florence Henderson. I also remember seeing *Saturday Night Fever*, which had just been released, and falling in love with John Travolta.

After the visits from the girls, I was alone again. I talked to Mike long distance every day in Crested Butte. His dad had given me his phone card to make as many calls as I needed. Our friends were so generous. Before we left for LA, Jeff Jacobson, a friend in CB, organized a fund-raiser for us and collected $800 for us. Patty Wesley organized a bigger party in Minneapolis and collected $3,200 for us. Having some extra cash really relieved some of the stress of the financial enormity of the situation. One day someone special showed up at the hospital. He appeared suddenly and unexpectedly. It was our old friend, Mark Tierney, who was an usher in our wedding and one of the old gang from Minneapolis. We had lost touch for a while, but now he was living in Santa Monica and working at Kaiser Permanente in LA. Mark saved me. "Ginny, we're going to check you out of your hotel today, and you're going to rent a car instead. I want you to come and live with me in Santa Monica. You'll love it there, and you can drive to the hospital every day."

That's exactly what I did, and he saved me from the tedium and despair of what I was having to do alone. He definitely became one of my special symbols in life. I adore Mark. He is an amazing giver and true friend. From that point forward I made steady progress in getting Page released from the hospital. I felt she was becoming demoralized from so many days in that sterile environment. The doctors wanted her to gain more weight. That would take forever. She never smiled. I decided to take her out. Dr. Pulec backed me up, but entrusted me with the care of her tracheotomy. It was a little scary to be the only one who could change and clean her trach. I learned exactly how to do it and called my parents to drive to LA to pick us up. Mark had supported me and fed me every night for a month. He was there every night to talk to me, laugh with me, and comfort me when I had to cry. He was a stand-up guy like no other. Mike came out once to visit, but he had to go right back to his job so we could keep our insurance.

The day we left the hospital I dressed Page all up and fixed her adorable half head of curly red hair. She began waving bye-bye to all the nurses and started smiling her crooked little smile. She was happy finally, and so was I. The rest was smooth sailing from the removal of the tracheostomy tube and feeding tube to learning to eat real food again. We had a real celebration on her third birthday, when she weighed 23 lb. Page is a true fighter and survivor, and she gave us so much joy with every little milestone she made. She started kindergarten in Crested Butte at age five. She learned to ride a bike that summer with Quana by her side. By then I had already met Sybil.

Sybil

Sybil was a beautiful magical gift the universe gave to me. She became one of my best friends as soon as I met her. She appeared at my new house on Butte Avenue at the edge of town one day. Mike and I had sold our first house, the coal-burning one, for twice what we paid for it two years later. We bought a lot with a spectacular view of Paradise Valley. No one could build across the street to impede our views because it was swampland. We built a great little two-story house and moved in right before the school year started. Sybil and Johnny had one little girl, Stacey, who was two weeks older than Page. Stacey, Page, and Quana became the famous little threesome in that amazing space in time that was Crested Butte in 1980. The streets were finally paved in town, and our lives were really a dream.

Sybil had heard my story with Page, so she came over to our house to meet me and ask what I thought about the tubes because Stacey was having ear infections. What a knockout she was. She was born in Tierra del Fuego in the very tip of Chile. Her parents ended up in Houston, where she grew up and married Johnny when she was sixteen much to her father's chagrin. She had been a ballerina and had all the material things that life had to offer. She fell hard for Johnny, and they were married when he was nineteen. A year later one of her younger brothers accidentally shot and killed himself at a pool party in their backyard. Her mother had a breakdown, and Sybil stepped in to be the matriarch of the family. She had one other brother and a baby sister. Sybil was the genuine article and completely unaffected. We became very close, and our girls felt the same way about each other. Pretty soon Page was spending more time at their house than ours.

Right about that time Mike's mom and dad came to Crested Butte for a visit. Mike and his dad went fishing or hunting, and I entertained Mary. They were both crazy about Page. Mary wanted to see what we had in the way of secondhand stores in CB. There wasn't much of anything except a really poor excuse for a place where one might look for a Halloween costume. She began telling me that it was the latest trend in the city, nearly new stores. What did we have for kids? Nothing. After Dick and Mary were gone, I couldn't get it out of my mind—a children's nearly new store. That was the birth of Mountain Moppets. Sybil and I became partners and received a $6,000 signature loan from the bank in Crested Butte. The loan officer took a chance on us. He couldn't resist our enthusiasm. We started with one hundred square feet on the second floor above a bike shop. Within a month we moved to the empty post office space on Elk Avenue. That space was two hundred square feet. Not long after that we signed a lease on a space across the street in a new building that was five hundred square feet. We were carrying new merchandise at that point and going to market in Denver. It was a passion for both of us. We agreed on everything. We had the same style in our taste for kids' clothes. We were both big-city girls grooving in a small town. Crested Butte had a population of 1,200 that swelled to 8,000 during the winter. I have so many vivid memories of the time we had together in the Butte. The Fourth of July Parade every year was riotous, and the girls loved dressing up for the festivities. One year we decorated Page's bike with red, white, and blue crepe paper, and she wore her Wonder Woman panties and tank top. She was so cute! Stacey actually got to ride in the parade in Johnny's old truck. Page and Quana probably jumped on too! Those little girls were golden in that town. Everyone knew them, and we felt they were safe to run free when they were five years old.

The other memory that is stellar in my mind was our rafting trip down the Delores River with all three girls. Lynette, Mark, Quana, Sybil, Stacey, Mike, Page, and I took off on an adventure that I will never forget. I think Johnny will always regret that he didn't make that trip. We headed south to Delores, Colorado, cars loaded with life vests, food, and camping gear. Mike and I owned a big raft, which we had painted silver because it needed to be sealed after all the wreaks we had in it. We could all ride together, with Michael being the captain and rudder man. He knew what he was doing, and all the rest of us could take directions. The little girls just needed to stay seated most of the time. We would be on the river three days. It was an easy, gentle float down the river in a deep canyon. The weather was perfect. Just hot enough to swim if we wanted to and the beer cans floating behind stayed cool in the river. The second night we camped at a beautiful site along the bank of the river. All three little girls stayed in a pop-up tent Mike and I had retrieved on an earlier trip down the difficult part of the river. The owners never appeared, so we left a note with our number at the general store in Delores. We used that tent many times over the years. The rest of us threw our sleeping bags on mats under a rock overhang a few yards away from the tent. Mark found a little scorpion in his sleeping bag. It stung him before he knew what happened.

When the sun came up, we all got up and ready to cook breakfast for all of us. You tend to get really hungry on the river. It was so windy that morning that we put big rocks on top of the flipped-over raft. It took some skill to build a campfire and cook pancakes and bacon and eggs for all of us. We were all helping when in the blink of an eye, the strong wind picked up our raft, rocks, and all, floated it high into the air, and flipped it over. We all watched as it landed right in the middle of the river and started floating away. Oh shit! This was a disaster! Three little girls and five adults in a deep canyon with no way out but the river! Mike lost no time getting into action, but he ran and jumped in the river with his sweatsuit on and immediately started to sink. Thank God, Mark assessed the situation correctly and ran down a rocky path along the river on his bare feet. *Pain*! He got far enough ahead of the raft that he was successful in grabbing a hold of it and bringing over to the shore. We all cheered and jumped up and down hugging each other well aware that we almost had a catastrophe.

My favorite memory with Michael was our cross-country ski trip to Elkton. What Michael taught me was to go outside my limitations. On this particular overnight trip we planned it to be during a full moon. We went with our neighbors and very close friends, Jackie and John. I fixed spaghetti and French bread to bring for dinner. They were in charge of breakfast in the morning. Now we were ready to go, and it was about 10:00 a.m. Lynnie was keeping Page overnight, so we had no worries. Michael asked me if I wanted to try a quarter tab of acid with the rest of them. He thought this would be the best possible scenario for taking a psychedelic substance—a beautiful sunny day with an untracked blanket of snow for eight miles in front of us. I would be in a line with the three of them. Michael and John would break trail, and Jackie and I would follow. He was meticulous about how much I put on my tongue. "You're a little bit of a wimp. I want you to have fun with this." "Okay, whatever you say, Michael. I trust you."

OMG, within a few minutes, I was seeing diamonds on the sparkling snow. I felt invigorated. I was breathing in crisp, clean oxygen. It was delicious. I had boundless energy. I kept up with all of them and was so happy and grateful that I lived in this exquisite place—perfect, pristine wilderness with no one else in sight, but us. We stopped for snacks. They were the best treats I'd ever had. We skied until dusk, and then we saw the cabins in the distance. They looked like hobbit houses all blanketed in snow with little white lights glowing where the windows should be. A puff of smoke was rising from the chimney. It was all ready for us, all toasty and warm inside. We fixed the spaghetti on the wood stove and had a couple of hits of pot. After a short rest, we put our skis back on and floated through the knee-deep powder until two thirty in the morning. I couldn't climb anymore. The next morning we cruised back to town as if our energy would never run out.

Michael Falls

One beautiful summer day while I was pulling my shift at Mountain Moppets, Tiger Mount came racing through the door with a look on his face that made me pause. "Ginny, you need to come right away. Mike has fallen off the roof!" "Oh no, let me finish up with these customers, and I'll be right there." The customers were lined up at the desk to make their purchases. "No, Ginny, I'm not kidding. You need to come *now*. It's really bad." I felt sick to my stomach, and a chill ran through my body as the adrenaline came pulsing through my veins. I asked everyone to leave the store, locked the door, jumped on my ten-speed bike, and raced over to the building where the crew was doing a roofing job. As I pulled up on my bike and jumped off throwing it to the side, I saw Michael lying on the ground with a lot of people kneeling around him. They made way for me, and I got down next to my husband and looked in his eyes. He looked at me with his beautiful expressive eyes and said, "Ginny, I don't want to be a cripple. Please."

The ambulance was already there with a lot of guys we knew. They did their job as EMTs, carefully getting Mike on a bodyboard and loading him into the van. I climbed in next to him and suffered with him during the long ride to the Gunnison Hospital. I was so scared now. They were telling me to keep talking to Michael. Don't let him pass out. Make him breathe. Don't let him panic. We all rushed into the hospital, and soon they were x-raying his back. His legs were stiff. We thought that was a good sign because if his spinal cord were severed, they would be limp. The helicopter was there. They wouldn't let me go with him. There wasn't enough room. I would have to drive three hours to Grand Junction. Someone drove me back to Crested Butte so I could get my car and see about Page. Lynette had Page and told me not to worry, just go. I grabbed a change of clothes and headed to Grand Junction in our Saab.

They couldn't wait until I got there to do the surgery. I sat in the waiting room all by myself. The minutes and hours dragged by. When the surgeon came to talk to me, he said, "He made it through okay, but you should prepare yourself for a wheelchair." "Is his spinal cord severed?" "No, but I don't think he'll ever walk again." Oh sure, just take all my hope away. Surgeons have no bedside manner or compassion in general. Dr. Pulec, Page's surgeon, was an exception to the rule. Now reality began to set in slowly. We certainly had all the support of our friends and family. We made the decision to have Michael's rehab at the University of Minnesota. All of his family was there, including nine brothers and sisters, nephews and nieces, family friends, and my brother Tom.

We sold our house in Crested Butte and moved to Minneapolis for six weeks of rehab. Mike was determined to get through faster. He worked really hard, and I was his biggest cheerleader. Page was Page and she brightened our days. She was a precious little six-year-old girl who loved to be part of every crowd whether it was her cousins, her grandparents, or my dear friends the Flashes. They all wanted her around and loved her and entertained her. Accepting the fate of a paraplegic was brutal. Think of everything you love in life and then being forced to give it up. Everything. The whole process of rehab was extremely depressing. It was very important to stay motivated. Michael was motivated, motivated to get out and back to Crested Butte. We moved back exactly six weeks later and lived for free in our friends', the Mounts, condo up on the mountain. Mike had a handicapped-accessible car that his father bought him and a four-wheeler to get around in the mountains if he wanted to fish or hunt. Mike was a survivor deluxe. He wasn't a happy camper, but he tried to be. His motivation carried him through the following winter when we decided to try living in Gunnison, one of the coldest places on the planet. It was miserable there, and Page started second grade in a classroom that had twenty-two students instead of the twelve she was used to in Crested Butte. During that winter Michael learned to tie fly's, my parents came for Christmas, my brother Tom survived a horrendous avalanche, and Mike decided to go back to school. I drove up to Crested Butte every other day to work at Mountain Moppets. I cried a river on that drive. A river. Thank the universe for Mountain Moppets. That shop saved me more than once when I felt sad and frustrated with what was happening to our lives. It was our own original creation, and our customers loved it. Sybil and I had created a successful business all on our own, and we could dress our girls in designer clothes every day.

Trying to understand why we had so many catastrophic events happen in a relatively short period of time confounded me. Why did we have so much heartache? Why did Mike survive Vietnam only to fall off the roof ten years later? Why, why, why. My heart ached all the time, literally ached. I was in pain. About that time a friend recommended that I see a particular psychic in Glenwood

Springs. I had always been curious about the metaphysical world. I wanted to try it. It gave me something to look forward to. Her name was Sheila Peterson. She is famous now because of Esther and Jerry Hicks's book titled *The Law of Attraction*. She channeled an entity named THEO. My first encounter with THEO changed the way I viewed Mike's tragedy.

Sheila was lying down on a sofa when our session began. THEO came through immediately. *It is the beginning is it not?* The voice was so strange. It sounded like a computer speaking, otherworldly. She told me that Mike had chosen this path and that I needed to take care of myself. I should go where there is water by myself or with a friend, not family. We should move closer to a city area; we could live in the mountainous area. Do you see? I should take time for myself. It is not selfish; it is selfless. She told me to utilize massage and body work. I would release much emotion in this way. Allow it to happen. You have been holding in too much energy. We would depart. God's love unto you. I saw Sheila one more time, and then we moved to Colorado Springs.

Colorado Springs

I found my paradise in Colorado Springs. Sybil and I managed to come to an agreement about Mountain Moppets. It was a little bit of a bumpy road, but best friends always find a way. She would own the store in Crested Butte, and I could open my own in Colorado Springs. She paid me an agreed amount, and I was able to secure a loan from State Bank and Trust in Plaza of the Rockies with my father-in-law cosigning the note. I had a lot of help from the design team in that controversial building on South Tejon with the skating rink inside. It worked right away with the help of my new friend, Becky. I met her at the Olympic Training Center volunteering for the U.S. Ski Association. We sat down together for lunch one day, and she asked me what I did, and then she told me she needed to get a job. Her kids were driving her nuts and vice versa. She had never worked retail, but she knew a lot of people. I hired her on the spot. Those were the magic words—*I know a lot of people.*

I was at market in Denver when we opened the doors for the first time. She ran it all alone that day. We made $200 and the Grand Opening was a few days later. Becky wrote personal notes to key people with kids. Broadmoor people. Bingo! Colorado Springs was very, very good to me. I was very compatible with the ice-skating rink in the center of the building. It was lots of fun to be in a new building that was modeled on the Galleria in Dallas. Many beautiful retail stores occupied that building in those early days, but things began to fall apart. We had very little business in the spring and summer. The windows were tinted too dark. Businesses started to fail. Mountain Moppets was becoming the anchor store on the first floor. I could see the writing on the wall. That's when I met Ruby.

Michael was in law school in Boulder by then, commuting home on weekends. I starting looking for another location for Mountain Moppets. Ruby owned a supersuccessful women's boutique in Old Colorado City. I had discovered that store and had purchased quite a few clothes there. I loved her energy, and she loved mine. I told her I was interested in moving, but I would have to break my lease at Plaza of the Rockies. She told me if I moved to OCC, I would never regret it. I trusted her. She had the Midas touch. I moved out of Plaza of the Rockies and broke my lease. I was set up in my new space at 26th and Colorado the next day. Women came in wanting to buy clothing out of giant black garbage bags that I had moved all the merchandise in. One gal spent $800 on stuff out of a black garbage bag! Go figure.

It was a good thing that the move turned my business into a very lucrative operation because I did get sued big-time for breaking my lease. I freaked out. The Bank of Nova Scotia, the second largest bank in Canada, sued me for all future rent and interest for the remainder of my lease. Mike knew I was scared and told me not to worry. He told me I made the right decision. It was a business decision. I hired a lawyer in Denver, and we tried to figure out what to do. The answer came to me one sleepless night when I was drifting off to sleep. What did these people want with me? They certainly didn't want to run a children's boutique. We had no equity in our home since we had just purchased it with gifted money from Mary and Dick. My husband was disabled and in law school with student loans pending. They still made me go through the incredibly stressful deposition process. I would share a ride with Jackie Kirk of Kirk and Hill women's clothing store, who was also being sued for breaking her lease. She had a different attorney in the same firm, so we comforted and supported each other through the whole ordeal. We have remained dear friends and confidants for many years. She is an amazing businesswoman and an extremely genuine person. I ended up settling with the banks for $5,000. I paid the attorney $5,000. The first month in my new location I made so much money that I was able to write them both a check. I had to really scramble to reorder enough merchandise to fill up the store.

The next eight years were magical for Mountain Moppets and me. My numbers went up, up, up every year. However, there were red flags that my marriage was starting to falter. I was happy, but Michael was not. He had demons that I could not really deal with. I thought that if I stayed positive I could overcome anything. I could not. Some things were way bigger than me. PTSD and a young life of abuse had created a big black hole in Michael, which I could not fill up no matter how hard I tried. I cried a lot and felt inadequate in many ways because I couldn't make him happy. He had a temper that was uncontrollable. It was getting worse, and it was taking its toll on me. I started having some very worrisome symptoms of tingling and numbness in my extremities. I started tripping quite a bit and my coordination was not so good.

I finally saw a doctor at Evans Hospital at Ft. Carson. He recommended I have an MRI, but I had to go off base to get it. I saw a neurologist, and he said the MRI was clear, but he gave a diagnosis of probable MS. Why? I grew up in Minnesota, where the incidence was higher, and the symptoms might indicate MS. In my usual fashion, I tried to blow it off. I just put it out of my mind. About that time my mom called me from California. She and my dad had been retired for twenty-two years at that time. She told me they wanted to help me while Mike was in law school. They wanted to know their only grandchild. Colorado Springs had a great climate and seasons. She missed the seasons. Most of their good friends were gone now. I was shocked. I didn't know if I wanted them to be around all the time. We hadn't lived near each other for many years. I knew she had made up her mind, and it really did make sense. They were pretty old to move, but I knew they had one more move in them. They came and sold their house in San Diego for four times what they paid for it. Now they would have a real nest egg. My mom wanted to rent an apartment with a view. They found one in a high-rise down the street from us on the eleventh floor. She called it a penthouse. It did have a beautiful view of Cheyenne Mountain, and they both loved it. Helen and Harold in Colorado Springs, imagine that!

My parents were a tremendous help to me, and we had many good times with the holidays and all Page's activities. My mom had so much pride in all of us. She always told me she could tell when some little kid was dressed in Mountain Moppets clothes at church. She was a practicing Catholic who picked and chose what she wanted from the religion. I had drifted away during the Vietnam War and was never coming back. My brother Tom was her only child who bought into The Church. My mother was a very happy, positive person who was a class act all the way and more. She was beautiful with her perfectly coifed pure white hair and elegant clothes. She loved shopping with me. I would make her treat herself because she deserved it. I loved my mom so much. She was beautiful inside and out, and she loved to hug—a complete giver and perfect example for a daughter and granddaughter. Page felt the same way about her. The two of them made each other feel special.

One day I was reading the Sunday paper and found an ad in *Parade Magazine* for handwriting analysis by Carlos Pedregal for $12.95. Here's what came in the mail ten days later:

Graphology
1744 Julia Goldbach Avenue, Ronkonkoma, New York 11779

August 30, 1990

022803321-9011-11
Ms. Virginia J. Wesley
1109 Parkview Blvd
Colorado Springs, CO 80906

Dear Ms. Wesley,

Thank you for responding to the handwriting analysis offer.

This computer-printed graphological analysis has been prepared by a team trained and supervised by Graphologist Carlos Pedregal.

Here is the result of your analysis, which is confidential, of course. The following paragraphs describe the dominant characteristics of your personality as reflected by your handwriting.

Respect

You possess a highly developed sense of respect: respect for society, for institutions, for human beings and, of course, for yourself.

You know how to elevate even the most menial undertaking.

The courtesy and interest you demonstrate to those who associate with you make your company unforgettable. Your concepts of life, of people, and of things help those who share your life to improve themselves, to respect others . . . and themselves as well.

But an acute sense of respect carries with it the danger of timidity. Do not allow yourself sense of respect to translate itself into an excessive delicacy when dealing with others.

Well-bred and Educated

You are well-bred, an uncommon feature in our day and age. Good manners rather than sheer force enable you to attain your goals.

Your unswerving correctness in all circumstances makes you an exceptional colleague, companion, or friend, and is the key to a professional and social success very few people achieve.

Well-balanced

From your handwriting, it can be observed that you have a sensible and well-balanced personality.

Even while involved in passionate discussions, you are capable of being fair-minded, of seeing the pros and cons of a problem, and of coming up with an accurate evaluation.

In general, your wisdom enables you to maintain a cool head and to find the middle ground, where the correct solution lies.

Strength and Vitality

You are an energetic person, always active, on whom one can rely. When you undertake something, you don't stop until you have finished. You are one of those lively people who never fail to animate those around them.

The dominant characteristics of your personality are strength, energy, and decisiveness.

Passionate

When it comes to feelings, you are somewhat of an extremist. Your passionate attitude has much to be said for it. But when passion is unrelenting, it has some drawbacks.

Passion alone does not allow you to fully develop your capacity to love. Your emotional relationships can suffer, and both you and the people with whom you are linked emotionally can be harmed by this attitude. Try to better channel your basic drives.

Overimaginative

You would do well to restrain your imagination from leaping over its boundaries, as it tends to do. It is tempting for you to use your imagination, your open intelligence, and your way with words to go beyond the facts from time to time.

By channeling your talents and adopting a more objective, more realistic approach, you can put these characteristics to work for you.

Self-control

Under trying circumstances, you manage to maintain your self-control because of your capacity to keep impulses from getting the better part of you.

You judge events accurately, but you must take care not to fall into authoritarianism.

Energy and Decision

In spite of all we have said up to now, you have an interior force that is always impelling you to move forward. Your gaze is fixed more on the future than on the past. You want to reach your goals, and you undoubtedly get to where you are going.

The above are fundamental characteristics of your personality, according to your handwriting. An analysis of the combination of these characteristics was carried out in order to determine the presence of specific tendencies of behavior. In your case, it did not reveal any particularly exaggerated tendency.

I hope you have found this analysis interesting and that is profitable to you.

We are all aware of how difficult it is to get to know ourselves. Before you make a definitive judgment on the results of this analysis, let your family or close friends read it. The opinion we have of ourselves frequently does not correspond to reality. We are generally either too self-indulgent or too critical of ourselves. And very often, even clear contradictions are inherent in us.

Thanking you for your confidence, I am,

Sincerely yours,
Carlos Pedregal

I have read that analysis many times over the years. It gives me comfort when I think I have lost my way. It makes me remember to hang tough and always trust my gut.

Somewhere in here we got a call that Mike's dad was dying of lung cancer. He was a two-pack-a-day guy his whole life. We flew back to Minneapolis. It took him two weeks to die. Mike had made peace with his dad because of the accident, thank the universe. Not many of the other kids had. I thanked him profusely for helping me in my business. He said he wouldn't have done if he didn't believe in me. I made good on the note with the help of my dad, Harold. He lent me the money to pay off the note because he wanted to. I never asked. My dad was a sentimental guy who loved me a lot. He once told one of the women in the nursing home he was in for a few months, "Everyone should have a daughter." Dick died a painful death in the hospital surrounded by his ten children. He impacted on all of their lives a great deal. He didn't love them all unconditionally, but I think he tried to be a good man in the end. Michael gave the eulogy and brought even the grown men to tears. Michael gave killer speeches from the heart.

Dick was able to see his son graduate from law school the year before, and he bought me a lobster dinner. "Have anything you want." I got food poisoning and couldn't make Mike's graduation party. Page and Mary and Dick went, but I had to stay in bed. I think Mike was mad at me, but I was too sick to care. Law school in Boulder didn't do much for our marriage. I'm pretty sure he was having an affair with someone in his graduating class. Mike passed the bar several months later and went to work as a district attorney for El Paso County. I was proud of him for staying so focused and finally making a real paycheck. He made friends easily, and I had fun meeting all the new people and promoting my business. I decided it was time to get into a nicer handicapped-accessible new house. We sold our house on Parkview and bought a new townhome under construction. Mike wasn't that much into it, but I was, so we went with it. Then he left me the first time. I was so devastated. I cried and pleaded with him not to leave, but he went anyway. We had sold our house, and the new house wasn't ready on time. I had to rent an apartment with Page, and it was such a hassle. I put all our furniture in storage and found a furnished place. Mike couldn't handle his hunting dog, Babe, so I had to take her. He informed me he was taking his half of the proceeds from the sale of our house to pay off school loans and his credit card bills. That made me think of the time we sold our first house and he bought a brand-new truck without even asking me.

Life sucked for a while after that. Thank the universe I had my business; it saved me many times from despair. I always loved going to work and unpacking boxes with beautiful merchandise and selling it. Page was hanging in there with high school, getting good grades, and freaking me out with piercing her nose and shaving her head at the nape of her neck halfway up. I felt she was establishing a nice group of friends who were mostly interested in art like she was. She was unique in her appearance and her heart. She was comfortable with her body image—tall and thin, but most importantly her asymmetrical face. She had overcome a lot of unkind teasing in grade school and junior high. The kids would ask her why her smile was crooked and her voice was like it was. Then they would twist their faces around in a contorted shape. All it took was one friend telling her she was special and beautiful because of her face, and she chose to embrace that. Mike and I would always tell her she had been beautiful her whole life, and everyone said so. It's hard for me to look at the surgery side of her face because it reminds me how hard she had to fight to survive that extremely unusual imperfection of nature. I have always believed it was Mike's exposure to Agent Orange in Vietnam. I may pursue that in the future. Page is my miracle girl. I am so blessed that she made it through such a high-risk surgery and has thrived and lived a normal life.

After three months of waiting for the new house to be finished, it was time to move in. Michael called me and indicated he was having second thoughts about leaving me. He said he was afraid he was losing me. Naturally, I asked him if he wanted to try again. We all moved in the completely accessible townhome before Page's senior year. Mike finished with the DA and had gone into partnership with a well-known criminal defense attorney in Colorado Springs. He was making more money now, so we started to think about traveling a little more. He planned a trip for us to the U.S. Virgin Islands. It was a remarkable kayaking adventure with a group of about twelve people with two guides who would prepare all the meals and provide all the camping gear. We kayaked between islands and then camped and explored those gorgeous spots. It was absolutely incredible kayaking in those pristine waters, and I found kayaking those long distances invigorating and challenging because I had to be the rudder person in the back. Mike's wheelchair was strapped outside the center of the kayak. That means I had to steer the kayak with my feet and paddle at the same time. Michael would be irritated with me because we weren't the first one in. He was competitive because he was always the best at everything before his accident. My favorite part though was sitting around the campfire at night drinking beer and eating the delicious food the guides prepared. Mike and Jim and I were the entertainment for the whole group. Jim was our disabled friend, the best man in our wedding, who was thrown from a car in a wreck about the same time Mike fell of the roof. He was in a coma for six months in Grand Junction and then miraculously woke up. He had severe brain stem damage, but he was rehabilitated to a point where he could walk with crutches. His speech was very difficult to understand, but if you took time to really listen, you would be amazed at how intelligent and funny he was. What an unlikely crew we were—two gimps and a tall and very attractive girl traveling as a threesome. At first I thought the other couples would be bummed out that they had to travel with a couple of guys who needed extra help, but they turned out to be the life of the party every day nonstop. Mike and I were not very close on the trip. It was kind of uncomfortable for me really because he seemed irritated with me most of the time. I noticed I would tire more easily and I was tripping and feeling uncoordinated a lot. He wouldn't make love at the end of the trip because we hadn't been intimate at all while we were sleeping in the tent. It was my fault because I just didn't feel like it. His temper had taken its toll on my libido and had been for a long, long time. I could see the writing on the wall. I didn't think we were going to make it.

Page started her senior year at Cheyenne Mountain High School and was accepted at CU, Boulder, so I was looking at becoming an empty nester. Mike bought a couple of kayaks, one blue and one pink. He started telling me he wanted to die, that he hated his life almost every day. He didn't like his job and was losing his temper a lot. His pain was becoming totally unbearable, and he thought he might be getting a pressure sore. My heart ached every day. There was no solution to this big problem. Overwhelming problem.

One day I was at work, and my cleaning lady, Linda, called in a panic on the phone. "Mike is here at the house with another guy, and they are taking things out of the house! They are taking the small TV out of your bedroom and all his guns!" "It's okay, Linda, they belong to him. Just stay out of his way and let him go." That was the last time he had to leave. I was emotionally exhausted. I had become a little tougher. He picked me up the next day on his lunch break. I was working at my second shop 360 Degrees, which I started with a former employee of Mountain Moppets. Her name was Basia. She was from Poland and very gifted and narcissistic, but we had a dynamic business there for a while. It picked up where Mountain Moppets left of. We liked to say we crossed the generation gap twice because we sold to teenage girls and boys, their mothers, and their grandmothers. When I got in the car with Michael, I started crying and telling him I couldn't go through this anymore. It was just too painful. He told me he was so sorry, but he had to leave; he was ruining my life. I would have never left him in a million years, but the truth was he *was* ruining my life. I couldn't separate myself from him, and he was pulling me right down in the abyss with him. In the end I chose life.

We agreed to keep our word and take Page and her friends to Lake Powell over summer break for her graduation gift. We would figure out how when the time came. Michael had hung in there until her senior year, but he needed to be on his own path. I needed to be on mine. When we split, my brother Matt was really sad. He said he thought Mike and I would always be together. So did I. When Mike and I finally agreed to divorce, it was swift. I was going to lose my health insurance because of his retirement status. He would quitclaim the house to me, because I had made the down payment with my half of the money from the house on Parkview we sold. He informed me I was entitled to half his settlement from Workman's Comp, which he would be getting when he turned fifty. But then he would be entitled to half of Mountain Moppets. I ended up with nothing but a large house payment and a house full of furniture that I had purchased with my own earned money from my business. He ended up with two kayaks, one little TV and his beloved guns. The day I went to sign the divorce papers in his office was one of the saddest days of my life. After I signed them, I sat on his lap in the wheelchair with my arms around his neck, and we both just wept. It marked the end of an era. The era of the golden couple, Michael and Ginny, who married for love, and they didn't make it after all.

Delphine, our French friend, came to visit and go to Lake Powell with us that summer. The kids drank many cases of beer and ate a lot of food. We rented a speedboat so they could all water-ski. Mike and I kayaked together, which was beautiful and sad. He seemed so flat. He was taking Zoloft and read a lot. That summer all of Page's friends hung out with me at the new house. I wanted them there because I didn't want to be alone. I hated being alone.

I still had my shop and my awesome friendship with Sybil. We continued to go to market at least three times a year. We both looked forward to those trips. Page and Stacey both went off to college in the fall. I was happy that Page was going to CU. I knew she would love it there. The next time we went to Dallas, I took our dog, Babe, with me and gave her to Mike's brother John. He had a German shorthair too and was willing to take her. Now I really was alone, but I had a lot more freedom. I was working out at World

Gym, figuring I might meet some men there. Instead I met a boy. He took me totally by surprise and sort of swept me off my feet. I wanted to get in shape for skiing, so I was thinking about hiring a trainer. David happened to be at the front desk when I inquired. He set me up with a trainer named Leo—a really great trainer. I would work with him three times a week. My body completely changed. I was forty-six, and Leo told me my body looked like a twenty-year-old. I liked that and I was feeling really good. I had had a boob job two months earlier. I was feeling pretty sexy. I'd always wanted boobs, and now I was free to do what I wanted with my own money. I have to say that men were paying a lot of attention to me. I'm pretty sure it was the boobs.

After a few times of seeing David when I came to the gym, he started hanging out around me. One night as I was leaving he asked if I wanted to go for a beer later. I had nothing else to do, so I said okay. He picked me up an hour later when he got off work. We went for a beer at Old Chicago on I-25. I had a big baggy sweater on and tight black leggings and boots. On the way home he put his hand on my leg and said my legs were in great shape. That surprised me because this guy was twenty-two. When he dropped me back at home, we had a very brief kiss. He called me when he got home, and we talked for an hour. I learned he was a hockey player and had inherited a lot of money when his mom died. He told me he had blown through most of it.

The next time I went to the gym he asked me if I wanted to rent a movie and watch it together when he got off work. We picked one out together. I remember it was a romantic thriller. It was romantic all right. About halfway through he made his move. I was drinking wine, and he was drinking beer. He kissed me on the neck. I told him I had to go to the bathroom, and when I came back, he told me he thought I was sexy. I fall for that kind of language. He was sexy too and very sure of himself. What the hell, I let my inhibitions go, and pretty soon we were in my bedroom. It was divine, what can I say?

I saw him for a few months, but I was meeting a few men my own age. David and I never socialized with anyone I knew. He was way too young to bring out in public. He was a cutie though and continued calling me even when he went away to school in Wisconsin. He even came into my shop one day, and I had to take him out in the backyard and tell him that I was intimate with someone my own age. He didn't care; he just wanted to be friends because he liked me.

After David there was Patrick who lived in Vail. We had sushi in Denver and saw a Rockies game. I visited him in Vail, and we played golf and visited his winery. That guy was irresistible. We weren't going to work because he wanted children, and I was done with that. He was irresistible though. Then there was Rick in Minneapolis. He was the ex of Karen who I went to Jamaica with. Mark and I went together for a second time, and Matt and Karen came along too. Anyway, Rick and I had some chemistry together, and he made a big play for me when I was visiting Mark in Minneapolis. He visited me in Colorado Springs after a brief phone romance. He called me rosebud and sweet pea on the phone. We went to Taos and played golf in Farmington, New Mexico, at the Point of the Pines four-star public golf course. That was amazing and I was a better golfer than he was. We had fun, so he invited me to St. Paul for the week after Christmas. He took me to a New Year's Eve party, and we were going to Karen's fortieth birthday. It all ended badly when he got jealous of my relationship with Mark. Rick had some issues, and I didn't want to deal with that. After that I had a dry spell for about two years, and then I met Dewayne.

Dewayne

Dewayne came into my life when I really needed a companion. I was so ready for male companionship that I turned to a matchmaker. I didn't feel that my chances of meeting a quality person were very high working in my shop all day. Donna the matchmaker was recommended to me by someone I don't remember. It seemed like a safe way to go because she personally screened each person she represented. I made an appointment and connected with her right away. She provided a fairly comprehensive questionnaire and interviewed me for about an hour. Then she informed me that three or four guys came immediately to mind for me. For $700 you would get seven matches: a match was only if you went out again after the initial meeting. I was anxious to get started, feeling this would be fun. I was wrong! She set me up with two different guys, and I have to say I squirmed both times because I was so uncomfortable. I didn't know how to say I wasn't interested without hurting the guy, so I just kept on talking until I was exhausted. I called her and said that I wasn't ready yet and that I wanted to take a break.

Sometime during this self-imposed break, I received an extremely disturbing call from Michael. He was in the psych ward lockdown at the VA hospital in Denver. He was on suicide watch. Page and I met at the hospital and went to the ward through metal gates. Mike wheeled in to the waiting room alone. We put our arms around his neck and hugged him. He told us he had played Russian roulette with one of his handguns and after about seven tries he gave up and drove himself to the hospital. That was an agonizing time for me. He was a broken man. Ara and I came back the next day, and she cut his hair because he had let himself go. He looked like the Unabomber. After a week, he pulled himself together and went back to his ranch in Alamosa.

I went on a fun trip to San Francisco with a couple of girlfriends, but I was feeling that emptiness again. When I returned home, I called Donna again. Another three months had passed, and I told her I wanted to try again. I explained further that I just didn't have any chemistry with the two guys before. She asked me how important looks were to me on a scale of one to ten. I said ten. She was surprised by that, but said she had a guy that she thought was really good looking and a sharp dresser. He was an attorney, and if I wanted to see what he looked like, I could look him up in the Yellow Pages because he had numerous pictures there. That sounded great to me. He didn't call for a couple of days, but when he did, I loved his voice on the phone. It was a beautiful deep-speaking voice like a radio announcer would have. We made a date for lunch the following Monday at Jake and Tilley's in Old Colorado City just a couple doors down from my shop, where I would be working. I could take a lunch break because I had an employee, Elaine, who could definitely handle things while I was gone. Then I would have an excuse to get back to work if I wasn't interested in him.

I started feeling nervous and sick about eleven thinking about meeting him. I didn't know how I felt about a guy named Dewayne. Elaine said, "Ginny, why don't you relax and try to enjoy yourself. It's only lunch." "Okay, what the heck." Walking over to the restaurant, I noticed what a gorgeous spring day it was with all the trees in full bloom. It was warm with no wind, and I felt a little excited to meet the face behind The Voice. The face was handsome, the teeth were perfectly straight, and he was well spoken and intelligent. This would work for me. After we finished lunch, we walked down the steps together and stood in the parking lot talking. I found myself hugging him and saying, "Well, what do you think? Is this a match?" "When can I see you again?" "I don't have plans for the weekend, so maybe then." "How about tomorrow?" I liked his style. We went out for dinner the next night at the Ritz downtown. He let me know his sensitive side right away. His sister had passed away from mouth cancer just two months earlier, and he was still raw. I saw the tears in his eyes while he was telling me, so he won my heart right then.

We were inseparable for the next few weeks, and then my sorority sister, Rebecca, from Alaska called and said she was going to be in town with her son, McCoy, and asked if they could stay with me. She brought a huge piece of king salmon with her and said I should invite a few people over for dinner and she would cook it on the grill. It was insanely delicious and a rare Alaskan-style wild salmon. Dewayne was there for dinner when she started to tell me I needed to plan a trip to Alaska because she and Michael, her husband, weren't going to be there forever. I decided right then I was going to take her up on the offer. We were alone in the den when she said I should bring Dewayne with me because I would have a lot more fun in Alaska with a guy. Dewayne jumped at the offer when I asked him, so we began planning the trip right then.

We landed in Anchorage, and Rebecca picked us up at the airport. It was so exciting to be on an amazing adventure with Dewayne. He was a fun guy who had a great zest and curiosity for life. On the way to Rebecca's house a moose crossed the road. I was stunned at how huge she was. If I stood next to her, I think my head would only come to the top of her leg. Rebecca had planned the entire trip for us. We took a train ride to Prince William Sound, and then a cruise to Valdez and then a high-end bus ride through some of the most beautiful scenery in the world. I found Alaska to be the most spectacularly beautiful Technicolor wonderland of royal blue water and sky, impossibly green trees, and snow-covered mountain peaks that defied the senses. That part of the trip took about five days, and then we were back in Anchorage for a few nights at Rebecca and Mike's. The next leg of the adventure involved driving McCoy's truck down the Kenai peninsula for a guided fishing trip and then further down to Homer at the very tip of what they called the Spit. Dewayne and I each caught a salmon. It was so fun even though the guide wondered if we wanted to keep them because they were only 12 lb. Give me a break, let a 12 lb fish go? Hey, we're from Colorado, dude! I was a little sleep deprived by the time we got to Homer because it never got dark enough for me.

Dewayne and I had an unfortunate incident in Soldotna, where we stopped to get our fish packed and frozen to take back to Colorado. Something insignificant I did irritated Dewayne, and he told me to shut up and get the fuck in the truck. *Whoa!* What did he say to me? That put a huge damper on the whole trip for me. I was mad for the rest of our stay in Alaska. I couldn't get over that. Then I spoke my liberal mind at a basically Republican conversation over dinner at Rebecca's the last night we were in Alaska. That's when I learned what a rabid Republican Dewayne was. I was anxious to get home because my eighty-six-year-old mom had had a hysterectomy while I was gone. I called Matt and found out it hadn't gone that well with my dad while she was in the hospital. I'll never know why she scheduled her surgery while I was going to be away. She was desperate I guess.

Helen

Dewayne and I broke up on the plane on the way home. It was unacceptable what he had said to me. It was a red flag for a guy who had never been married. When I got home my mom was a different person. Her voice had changed; it was lower and slower. My dad went in a temporary nursing home that apparently had no air-conditioning or TV. He just crashed there. My brother did the best he could, but I should have been there. My mom was better once she got home and had some nursing help coming in so she could rest. Pretty soon she was up and walking up and down the halls of her building, trying to regain her strength. It was slow going. I took her to her doctor appointments and she was totally healed from the surgery, according to him. She was depressed from the medications and anxious about my dad. He was absolutely dependant on her for everything. He wasn't able to fix a can of soup; he was so feeble.

I went with her to her doctor and mentioned she had anxiety. He put her on Prozac along with the Klonopin for her jumpy legs. That sealed her fate. She collapsed in the apartment. I got a call from her while I was at work. She was back in the hospital. I went there as soon as I closed the shop. I found her sad and agitated. "What do the doctors say, Mom?" "They say I can't go home until I put your father in a home. I can't take care of him anymore." "Well, mom, I've thought that for a long time. It's time." "Okay, honey, but you take care of it. I can't do it. I'll talk to him, but you make the arrangements." She was home the next day.

I had already looked into getting my dad into Cheyenne Mountain Nursing Home because I had heard it was lovely and it was only a block from my townhome. My parents had bought an insurance policy for long-term care and had been paying the premiums for years. My dad would have to be admitted with an injury or a need for therapy in order for Medicare to pay for anything. It was all doable. When I called my mom to tell her I had it all set up for dad, she said she had changed her mind. "Why Mom?" "I can't do it to him. He said he would never forgive if I put him in a home." I couldn't argue with her; she had made up her mind.

I woke up to the phone blasting in my ear. It was six in the morning. "Hello." "Ginny, your mother's gone over the wall!" My world started spinning. "Mrs. Wesley, this is officer so-and-so, and I'm with your father. There's an ambulance here for your mother. I'm afraid she jumped off their lanai." "Oh god, I'll be right there!" Then I did something I've never done before. I screamed a primal scream. The feeling of permanent loss penetrated my whole being. I was frozen. I couldn't think. McCoy came running upstairs from the lower level in his boxers. He was spending a few nights with me. He had been kicked out of Fountain Valley High School for drinking with friends in his room. "What's wrong, Ginny?" "My mom has committed suicide. I can't drive, McCoy. You have to take me."

I went in my walk-in closet and started shaking. I couldn't get dressed. I couldn't decide what to wear. Somehow I put some baggy shorts on and a big T-shirt. McCoy was in my car waiting for me. He was seventeen and had just experienced a suicide through me. We are connected for life even if I never see him again. I was able to direct him to my parents' apartment, and we saw the ambulance as we pulled up to the front entry. We parked the car there. He put his arm around me and walked me to the elevator and up to their apartment, where the door was open and two policemen were waiting for me. I told McCoy to take my car and do whatever he needed to do and then take a cab to the airport. Both of my brothers were unavailable. Tom was out of the country on a ski trip in Chile. Matt was with Ara, his new wife, on a road trip in Colorado. I asked where my dad was, and they pointed to the bedroom. My dad was in the bathroom brushing his teeth. "Your mother had a lot of guts. I wish I did." I put my arm around him and gave him a hug. I helped him get dressed and then I went out to the living room to talk to the policemen. I sat at the table and noticed she had left a note just as they were telling me. I read the handwriting I was so familiar with. The note was addressed to me, and I understood what she was saying about not being able to stand it anymore and to please understand. I did. She said she knew I would take care of my dad. She loved us all so much. All I could think about was calling Dewayne. I wanted Dewayne.

He answered the phone on the second ring. "Dewayne, my mom has committed suicide, and I need you to be with me, okay?" "Oh, Ginny, I'm so sorry. I'll be there in a few minutes. Hang on." I walked out on the lanai and saw a coffee cup on the floor next to a patio chair. I picked it up and saw it had what looked like a bunch of M&M's in the bottom. It was all her pills. She emptied all her pills in the bottom of the cup and then poured her coffee on top and drank it. Then she flew off the eleventh floor of the building. She did have guts. My mom was the most beautiful person I have ever known. I would miss her so much. No one ever loves you like your mother. She stayed in control of her own destiny. Michael called me to express his sadness over my mom's death a few days later, before the memorial. He told me she had written him a letter before she died, telling him how much she had always loved him. Helen loved Michael more than she did her own sons. She was able to communicate with him in a way she never had known from her own two boys. I always knew that because she had told me how she felt about Mike. She adored him. It killed her when we divorced, but she knew it was the best thing for me.

Dewayne did come right away, and we were together for another ten years. My dad went to the nursing home, and it was a disaster for him. After a few weeks I realized it was all about the beautiful lobby, but behind the scenes it was ugly and impersonal. Before I knew what was happening, all my dad's beautiful golf shirts and sweaters had disappeared, and he was dressed in clothes that didn't fit. I told the nurses that I would do his laundry, but it was too late. None of his clothes were ever found. They bathed him only once a week, so pretty soon he started to smell of urine. He would only eat a few bits of his food even when I came and ate with him. I was starting to worry about him all the time. That's when the angel, Lucille, came to see me at Mountain Moppets.

Lucille had been a great customer of Mountain Moppets when her kids were young or I should say her grandkids. She raised them when her own daughter failed as a mother. I hadn't seen her for a few years, but now she appeared again out of the blue. What an incredible human being she was. She had a calling in life. Her calling was stepping in and saving elderly people when their families were desperate. My dad went to live in her group home and thrived. I had to fight the nursing home to get him out because they wanted his money. Lucille charged the same amount as the nursing home, and the care was custom designed for him. She removed him from all the medications and insisted we dress him in designer sweat suits. She took pride in her people. If my dad wanted a fish sandwich from McDonald's every day, he got it. My dad lived another two and a half years after my mom died. He died in her home just as she promised he would. He was holding her hand and had eaten a miniature Snickers bar, and then he closed his eyes and passed away.

Life after Fifty

I inherited one-third of their estate, which wasn't large, but it was nice to have a chunk of money in the bank. I sold the townhome and moved in with Dewayne. I helped him gut and redecorate the ranch-style house he had purchased in the Skyway subdivision of Colorado Springs. Dewayne and I turned out to be good business partners. We bought the Mountain Moppets building together, and he moved his law practice from downtown to the second floor of the building in Old Colorado City. It worked out very well for him, and he had a view of Pike's Peak from his office.

Life with Dewayne could be magical. That guy had a lot of love to give. I was lucky to be the recipient. On my forty-ninth birthday he gave me the gift that kept on giving. I went to work that day, August 11, with Becky, my manager and one of my best friends at the time. About eleven I got a call telling me to be outside in front of my shop in a few minutes because a limousine would be there to pick me up. The handsome driver opened the door, and I slid in with Becky waving bye to me. There was a card on the seat, and it had a sweet sentiment telling me I was going to Nice and Naughty and I should pick out anything I wanted in the way of lingerie. I had a time limit of about ten minutes. So fun! Then I was back in the limo for the next stop downtown at a gourmet wine shop. A couple bottles of wine and some beautiful chocolates were waiting for me. I was back in the limo and on to Gentry's Flowers for an exquisite bouquet of roses. I was overwhelmed and kept feeling this was too much money, but that was just the beginning. Next stop was a spot where we could have

Virginia Jean Wesley

a hot tub after my hour-long massage. The limo disappeared, and
Dewayne showed up to join me. After our hot tub we went back
to the house for a catered dinner from the Picnic Basket. We ate
out on our beautiful patio, enjoyed the wine, and then the grand
finale—a Biggest Big Bertha golf club. He spoiled me that way for
our entire relationship. Dewayne believed in quality all the way. It
didn't mean we were always happy.

Dewayne really tried to make me happy, but there were fundamental
differences in our personalities and beliefs. We were both from
the graduating high school class of 1967. We grew up together
during the crazy 1970s. He went to KU, and I went to CU. Our
experiences were very different however. I was married at twenty
and stayed that way for twenty-five years. He never married, and
there were no children. Therein lay the biggest problem. I had
a lifetime of baggage and I was liberal. I was a big-city girl. He
was from a town in Kansas where the population was 1,200 and
he was conservative. Our time together was filled with beautiful
travels and beautiful cards that he gave me on all special occasions
usually accompanied by red roses. He was the most generous man
I have ever known—sometimes to a fault. He was generous in every
way except his ability to love outside of me. He had a hard time
opening up outside his relationship with me. Sometimes he gave
love and then withdrew it. I consider it a tragic flaw. My daughter,
Page, suffered because of it. There were other members of my
family that were hurt. I loved everyone in his family, and they loved
me back.

My family opened up to him, really loved him. He just didn't want
that many people in his life. I had a huge circle of friends and family.
That was always a problem. I couldn't change that. I loved all my
people. He did not. He tried though. Page really loved Dewayne.
She was away at CU in those early years of our relationship. He
was very generous with her. We would visit her in Boulder, and
he would always treat for dinner, oftentimes with her friends too.
When she graduated, he came to the party Michael and I hosted
and bought one of the paintings from her presentation. He was
the first to reach out to Mackie, Mike's wife, by giving her a hug
before we all went in to the restaurant.

84

After graduation, Page lived with her boyfriend in a cute little house in Denver. It was located on the border where underprivileged met rich. I think she was happy then because he was in art school and she had a job at the BMOCA—the Boulder Museum of Contemporary Art. She was all about art and always wanted to work around it. Dewayne and I were spending our free time golfing and biking and traveling. Some of our favorite spots for four-day weekends were Taos and Santa Fe. He loved to get a massage at a spa, and we both loved the local Mexican cuisine. We had a lot of things in common. It was nice. He always tried to make things special, and they usually were.

A mother's worst nightmare almost became a reality for me with a phone call from Page early one Saturday morning. "Mom, I don't want you to panic, but I was robbed at gunpoint last night. We couldn't go home because Dan gave him our keys, so we're at Bethany's in Boulder." "Oh god, what actually happened, Page?" She explained that a black man approached them in the alley behind their house late the night before as they were getting out of Dan's van. He wanted money, and of course, they only had a few dollars. Page told Dan not to talk to him, and the guy turned to Page with a gun and then hit her in the face with it. Dan kicked him to the ground, and a big knife flew out of his pants. Page was screaming at them both, and then the black guy grabbed the gun, stood up, and held it to Page's head. He told them both he was going to kill her. "Mom, I just looked down at my feet, and I don't remember anything after that. I guess I went somewhere else. I guess Dan begged and pleaded for my life and then told him he should take all the camera equipment because he could hawk it at a pawnshop for real money. Then he gave him the keys to the van, which had our house key too." "Oh shit, Page, are you sure you're all right?" "I am, Mom, I actually am just fine. It was so scary though, and Dan's pretty shook up." "Dewayne and I will drive up as soon as we get dressed." When the reality set in that I could have been the mother of a murdered daughter, it was a very sobering thought. How many lives did Page have? Turned out to be many.

We took everyone out for lunch, and it was determined that the two of them would stay with Dan's mom until they could find another place. The landlord ended up letting them out of the lease. The police never found the guy or any of the stolen equipment. The value was about $5,000, and I think Dan's father helped cover it because there was no insurance. It belonged to Dan's Art School. That was not the end of it for Page. She ended up in the hospital many times over the next few years, and her relationship with Dan ended, but it took a long time. She was diagnosed with PTSD and had a lot of free counseling and therapy courtesy of the city of Denver. Thank goodness I had paid for her health insurance after college because she couldn't stop vomiting and she was back in the hospital time and time again. I felt like I was reliving her childhood, and it was taking its toll on me. She was losing so much weight that she was starting to look anorexic.

After recuperating at our house, she couldn't wait to get back to Denver and her friends. Dewayne and I helped her move into a crummy apartment in downtown Denver. She was going to live alone and work her new job at the Denver Museum of Contemporary Art. She needed to have all four of her wisdom teeth pulled, so I paid for an oral surgeon who would sedate her. All four were impacted, and the doctor put her on vicadin with ibuprophen every four hours for pain. She seemed to be doing well and started back to work. I was happy to be leaving town with Dewayne on a trip to San Diego and meeting friends who were renting a house in La Jolla. It was always good for me to escape from my business and my twenty-five-year-old child for some R & R.

After spending the day at the beautiful Hotel del Coronado, Dewayne and I returned to the house we were sharing with our friends, Judy and Bentley, only to learn that Michael had called and left a message for me that Page was in Denver General. She needed emergency surgery for a perforated ulcer, and he was driving to Denver to be with her. Dewayne and I were on a flight out in the morning. Before we left I knew that ulcers happened if you had a certain bacteria in the stomach. Judy's dad was a physician, and I spoke to him long distance from Sacramento. We flew into Denver, and I went straight to the hospital. Mike was there, and Page had tubes down her throat and IVs running. She was a mess. The surgeons had cut her open from stem to stern. What was a small crosslike scar on her stomach from when she was two had turned into a jagged ugly swath from her sternum to her pubic line. Oh, Jesus, what my daughter had to endure. We almost lost her again. Her friend, Dan's cousin, had come to her rescue when she called him and told him she was in trouble. He picked Denver General, the indigent hospital, because it was the closest. He and the emergency-room doctors saved her life. The surgeons just kept spraying water and cutting because the contents of her stomach were spilling out into the body. So close, so scary. In her usual form, Page was a little testy with the medical staff. It's because she's a fighter. She's had to be. She ended up back on the couch with Dewayne and me.

Definitive Diagnosis

Page continued to have problems with her stomach off and on for a long time. She was so thin that I worried about her all the time. I was afraid she might not make it. I started seeing a psychologist and went on Zoloft for about two years. It helped me cope with my own issues. After Page's rounds in the hospital, I started having a lot of anxiety and burning sensations in my ankles. I decided I should see a neurologist again. I asked one of my customers at Mountain Moppets whose husband was a doctor if he could recommend a good neurologist. My last neurologist, Patricia Blake, had given up her practice in Denver. She told me her son had committed suicide the last time I saw her. She also told me that if I did have MS, it was the mildest case she had ever seen. My MRI was inconclusive. She thought she saw one hot spot on my brain. My customer's husband recommended Dr. Patricia Fodor who was with the big group of neurological associates in Colorado Springs. She was a new hotshot who claimed to specialize in multiple sclerosis. She scheduled me for an MRI right away. That was the beginning of my demise.

The test results came back. Dewayne and I went to the appointment together. Dr. Patricia Fodor decided she should show us the films from my MRI on a lighted screen where all the personnel were working. She threw the films up on the screen and said, "Look at all this white stuff. That's MS. Look at all this black stuff here. Those are *black holes* in your brain, and your brain is *shrinking*. You need to get on medication right away or you will become seriously disabled." I felt sick to my stomach. I was absolutely devastated. Up to that point I held hope that I didn't have MS. Now I had a definitive diagnosis. She took us into her office. I didn't like her manner. She was rough around the edges. She piled a bunch of DVDs in front of me and said I should watch them and then call her physician assistant and tell her which one I wanted to be on. No explanation of any of them; she wanted me to choose. Then she left the room, and on the way out, she said to Dewayne, "My, you are a good-looking man." Fuck her. How dare she hit on my boyfriend. Bitch! Dewayne and I walked out to the car, and I started to cry. He put his arms around me and said he was so sorry. Knowing Dewayne, he may have cried too, I don't remember. At that point I decided I shouldn't hide it anymore. I should tell people. The nurse practitioner called me several times pressuring me to choose one of the ABC drugs—Avonex, Betaseron, Copaxone. "You have a large lesion on your neck. It's very serious. You need to start right away." "I will never go on those drugs. I know what they do. They systematically destroy your immune system." "Well, that's all we have for MS."

Sometime after that Dewayne and I got married. I had been away for a few days on a buying trip to Dallas, and when I got home, he asked me to marry him. I wasn't all that keen on getting married, but he really thought he wanted to marry me. He had the wedding all planned. We would get married in Vegas, where his mom and dad had been married after WWII at a little chapel called Wee Kirk of the Heathers on the strip. He made reservations at the Venetian and had booked tickets for Celine Dion. We had awesome seats in the middle about ten rows back from the stage. Dewayne always did everything first class. He also arranged a helicopter flight to the Grand Canyon catered with champagne and lunch. We sat on the banks of the Colorado River with a few other couples and took in the view and drank the bubbly. I loved the flight. It was spectacular. We always had fun together, and he was very romantic. I don't know if I appreciated him enough. I always felt like there was something missing. There was. We were not sexually compatible. Who knows why that happens; it just does. You can try to say that that's not the important part, but for me that's the most important part, and I never really had it. I always have yearned for that.

Taylor and the Wedding

You know what saved Page in the end? Having a baby. Her name is Taylor. She saved me too. Page met Chas, and he could cook, so he was able to put a little weight on her while they were falling in love. There was a business failure that I foolishly bankrolled and lost most of my savings, but we had a beautiful outdoor wedding on August 28 five years ago. I had to move forward and not dwell on that business loss because what else can you do? Taylor was born on May 29 five years ago. She was three months old at the celebration of life/ wedding we held at Hillside Gardens in Colorado Springs. I was in heaven with my new granddaughter. The wedding was spectacular if I do say so myself. It had rained every weekend that summer, which was good because it was so green, but scary because we had two events planned that weekend. Sybil and Stacey came to the dinner Dewayne and I hosted at our house. We had all been to Stacey's wedding the weekend before at their ranch east of Gunnison. It was equally as spectacular. We all rode on hay wagons out to the river on their property and watched Johnny walk his only daughter down the wide path that had been mowed through the waist-deep hay. Stacey wore a princess strapless wedding dress and, Johnny wore his best cowboy hat and boots. Sybil was fighting breast cancer a second time fourteen years after the first, and I knew she wasn't going to make it, but in her usual style she made that wedding very special.

Every one of Mike's brothers and sisters came to Page's wedding except Mickey, Julie, and David. Patty, along with Tracey, her oldest daughter, was the wedding planner. All of their hard work made for a relaxed and truly enjoyable time for the mother of the bride. Our dearest Crested Butte friends were there. Also present was a large Minneapolis contingent, including Michael's mom and siblings, Mark and Jimmy, Kimmie and Nancy, my brother Tom and his wife, Diane, my cousin Pat and his wife, Paula. Jill, now a judge, performed the wedding vows and brought her two daughters Besse and Emma. Page had been the flower girl in Jill's wedding over twenty years earlier. Meggie came from Scottsdale with her friend Minnie, and my cousin Barbara came from Chicago. My special friend Judy was there from Denver with her husband, Barry, and daughter Tessa.

A miracle moment

Ginny and Dewayne

Page and father Michael

Page and Meggie at wedding

Page's wedding

The redheaded bride

The aunties had decorated Taylor's stroller with tulle and satin and a bunny skin that she lay on, and my niece, Nikki, and my nephew, Gustavo, pushed her down the aisle. The bumpy path made the baby cry, but it just added to the sweetness of the twilight ceremony. Cheyenne Mountain was the backdrop as Michael pushed his wheelchair down the aisle with his only child. We all cried at a sight many of us thought we'd never see. Mike had been in the wheelchair for twenty years. We are a family of survivors, that's for sure. After the ceremony everyone refilled their drinks at the bar, which was a funky old white bus, and headed over to the pavilion for a sit-down buffet dinner catered by Front Range Barbeque.

It was a fun and romantic wedding with a fire burning in the fireplace and the Rocky Mountains in full view. There were quite a few toasts by family and friends until I took over and thanked everyone for coming and then I passed the microphone to Michael the master speechmaker and father of the bride. His speech, as always, was so meaningful and memorable. He started out telling everyone how amazing it was that people came from all over to this wedding, got on plans and flew across the country to be there, how much that meant to our family. And then he raised his glass and toasted the highest power of all, the *power of love*!

Dewayne had disappeared for a while. I hadn't seen him for at least an hour, maybe more. Nikki and Gus asked me why we weren't dancing. I looked for him and then all of a sudden he appeared out of nowhere. The limousine had arrived and was ready to take the bride and groom and Taylor to their hotel. Dewayne had paid for that extra special touch. We all waved good-bye in the parking lot. Later in the car on the way home Dewayne told me that he couldn't take anymore of the wedding and my family and friends and that he went home for a while. Later I told him the wedding was the best day of my life. He told me it was the worst day of his.

Divorce was swift again when we decided it wasn't going to work. Once Dewayne said to me, "Ginny, you need a lot of people around you to make you happy. I'm not like that. I only need one." Splitting up isn't pleasant, and I never seemed to leave with more than I came in with. There was no point in claiming common law for ten years with Dewayne even though we owned two properties together, Mountain Moppets, and a house in St. George, Utah. He, being a lawyer, would fight me tooth and nail on that one. Besides, I didn't really feel I was entitled to any of his retirement money. I had my business and owned half of both properties.

I couldn't seem to find the right living situation after the divorce. It was hard being the one moving out. I bought a new condo with two thousand square feet because it required no money down, but I couldn't really swing the payment by myself, so I rented the downstairs to Page and Chas and baby Taylor. It seemed like a good plan for all of us. We each had our own totally separate large space. The big problem ended up being the kitchen, which we had to share. I had totally different standards than they did being a generation apart. I wanted the dishes done before I went to bed, and they wanted to do them in the morning. I was a neat freak, and they had a baby. Chas was a slob; Page wore herself out trying to please me. The best part for me was spending every morning with the *adorable* Ms. Taylor. She would crawl up the twelve stairs in the morning with Page behind her, and when she arrived at the top, she would flash a big, beautiful smile at her Gigi. *Total love fest*! I will always cherish that special time I had with her. It wasn't enough to keep me from fleeing the situation and running back to the serenity of Dewayne. I was so tired all the time. It was too much for me. Before everything fell apart though, I took a dream trip to Peru with Patty and Dan to visit Tracey, their daughter and Page's cousin. It was a trip I had always wanted to take. We went to Machu Picchu by train and then bus and finally hiking. I brought a cane, and with the help of everyone I was able to get to the top. That was something Mike and I should have done if things had turned out differently. It's hard to describe the sensation one gets being in an ancient place like that. It was an experience of a lifetime being in the Andes and staying in the magnificent town of Cusco at ten thousand feet.

Back at Dewayne's I became increasingly stressed because of my financial situation. I put the condo up for sale just one year later, which meant the kids had to face reality and get into something they could afford. They were in a panic, but ended up buying a house. I put Mountain Moppets on the market and played the waiting game. I was really having a hard time working full days. I didn't have any stamina, and I felt the MS was getting worse, maybe even progressing. I just couldn't work that hard anymore. Selling my business was one of the hardest and most stressful things I have ever done. The business broker tried to convince me it was worth less; my accountant assured me it was worth more. I loved my accountant, Paul. He took excellent care of me, and I trusted him above all others.

In the final negotiations I got the price I wanted, and I sold it to the right person. She loved it as much as I did and put it online. Mountain Moppets.com. Tracey was a tech person, and she designed the entire Web site herself. It was my dream that my baby, my original creation, would live on.

Sybil Passes Away

That winter I went to Crested Butte to see Sybil. She was not doing so well. She had lost all her hair again, but she was wearing a warm hat and still working at Oohs and Aahs, a decorating store in Gunnison. She was invaluable to that business. They didn't know what they were going to do without her. Stacey took over after Sybil died. I stayed overnight with her and Johnny at the ranch that cold January. A fire was going in the fireplace, and Sybil wanted to lie on the floor. I sat in the comfortable overstuffed chair and tried to reminisce about the fun times we had spent together over the years. It was peaceful talking with her. She told me she wasn't afraid to die. It was only the pain she was afraid of. Who wouldn't be? In the morning she came out in overalls. She said none of her clothes fit anymore because she was so bloated. She was still going to work.

Johnny called me late one night in March and said he thought she only had a few hours left. She was delirious. We talked quite a while. He seemed to be comforted by me. He comforted me because I knew he loved her so much. He called me late the next morning and said she was gone. She was holding his hand when she died. We both cried. I was so sad. Stacey called me a few days later. She told me her mom wanted to have her ashes buried in the spring at the ranch when it would be warm and people could wear bright colors and there would be flowers.

On a warm spring day in May over a hundred friends and family gathered at the ranch to remember Sybil and her beautiful life. Some of us had made memory boards in her honor. Johnny keeps the one I made inside the house. It was a lot of pictures of the two of us with our girls and on buying trips over the years. Stacey had asked me to speak because I was her mother's best friend. I wore a bright pink coat and jeans in her honor. As I stood in front of many old friends and acquaintances, my little granddaughter, eighteen-month-old Taylor, walked over to the hole in the ground where a tree had been placed in Sybil's honor. She crawled down in the hole, so I motioned Page to come and get her. Stacey came to me and said to please let her play in there because her mom would love that. So I began what I wanted to say:

We are all here to celebrate Sybil's life and in doing so I hope each of us in our own way can heal from the sadness we feel that she is gone from us in her three-dimensional being. My memories of Sybil began in 1978 when she was about twenty-seven and I was about thirty. I think she pulled up at our house on Butte Avenue, jumped out of her truck, and introduced herself to me. Someone had told her that Page had ear problems, and she needed someone to talk to because Stacey was having ear infections too and she was worried. I thought she was so lovely and beautiful. Instantly we became friends, and as I look back, I realize now that our meeting was one of the defining moments of my life. What started out as a simple friendship between two young women both with daughters born just three weeks apart became a deep and spiritual relationship that grew for over twenty-five years. Sybil and I and Stacey and Page set out on a life journey together. I have to say we squeezed out as much fun as we possibly could afford and sometimes even more than we could afford. Of course, as many of you might remember, Mountain Moppets was the beginning. With only a $100 investment each we together created Mountain Moppets Children's Boutique. For me, it has been my life's work. It has always been a labor of love, never seemed like work, provided us with wonderful fun trips and wardrobes for Stacey and Page and now my granddaughter, Taylor. The Crested Butte store opened in 1980 in the old post office on Elk Avenue. I am flooded with the most magical memories of our life in Crested Butte. Memories before the streets were paved, Honeydew's Nursery, The Bakery Café, talent shows at Crested Butte Elementary, Bobbi Reinhardt's dance classes. Stacey and Page were together in every picture, and Sybil and I were always together. So it went for those few magical, perfect years. Then one beautiful summer day Thornton Mount came into Mountain Moppets while I was working. Mike had fallen off the roof at Johnny's project. Lives so interwoven. We had to be ripped and torn away from Crested Butte, our perfect life. Sybil's and my relationship became deeper and richer. Our friendship was strong enough to survive a split of our business and best friends living apart. Perfect match as business partners, perfect match as friends. One often looks for their soul mate in a man, but I found it in a friend.

Her ashes were put in the ground with the tree. A giant wind came up as if to say, "Go home everyone. We're all done here." Everyone and their vehicles were gone in a matter of moments.

I moved out of Dewayne's house and in with my dear, dear friend and mentor Ruby a month later. I stayed with her while I closed on my new little house. I also closed on the business at the same time. My money situation loosened up, so I planned a celebration trip to Kauai for all of us—Page and Chas and my grandchildren. My sister-in-law came along too for a little Mexican spice. We all had an incredibly fun time. I rented a house that we had stayed in way back in 1979. Only this time it was bigger and better because the original one was destroyed in one of several hurricanes that hit Kauai. At that time Page had recovered from her surgery, and we met our friends Judy and Tim there for a week. The house both times was right on the beach. Exquisite. We fell asleep to the sound of waves on the shore. Taylor was the queen of cuteness in her bikini, and Baby Griffin slept under an umbrella. He was nine months old. Baby surfers. I was present for both my grandchildren's birth. Each one took an hour just like Page did. We were lucky that way, mother and daughter. That trip was the end of fun for me. When I came back the shit started to hit the fan.

I moved into my new house with a payment I could afford, but several networking businesses I was working pretty hard at just fell apart. I had unrealistic expectations for what I thought I could earn. I had no energy, and my MS symptoms were getting worse, actually shockingly fast. I just couldn't work very much; I was exhausted all the time. My friends in Minneapolis knew I was becoming depressed and worried about me. Nancy bought me a plane ticket, so I forced myself to go, but it was an incredible effort. The next year is a blur, but I know I leaned on Dewayne and Page a lot. I would see Dewayne on a regular basis. I know he was worried about me too. Matt would stop by every week and take me to lunch. He seems to always pull through when I need him. One day we drove up somewhere on the mountain and scattered Harold's ashes. I lost track of time.

I needed a refill on my bioidentical hormones, so I called my favorite Dr. Juedersonke. He would always try to help me with my depression and listen to my concerns about the MS. I received a letter from him telling me he could not refill my hormones unless I got a mammogram. Did I not get a mammogram this year? I'd had one every year religiously since I was forty. My mom had breast cancer twice, the first time when I was a year old. Well, of course, I would get a mammogram; it had been eighteen months. I called his office and told them it was scheduled, so he wrote me the prescription. I felt my breasts, did a self-breast exam, and did find some funny ridgelike lumps around the nipple. What the hell? How could I have not noticed that? I went for the mammogram and pointed out the ridges to the tech. She wasn't alarmed, but said the radiologist would review my films before I left. I waited in the exam room until someone came back. It was a long time. When the door opened, it was the radiologist, and he was very concerned. He thought I should have an ultrasound before I left. That looked troublesome too. He recommended I have a biopsy at Memorial Hospital. Now I was starting to get scared. When I got home, I called Dr. J., and his best advice was to call a breast specialist. He gave me two names. One was Ingrid Sharon. I called her right away because I knew her. She was a customer of mine at Mountain Moppets. She was an angel to me, maybe my guardian angel.

I was pulled off my hormones cold turkey and scheduled for an MRI four weeks later. Why so long? The hormones affected the films. I started spending weekends with Dewayne. It was nerve-racking, and my MS was flaring up. I had zero energy. We tried to take the grandkids for a day, and Dewayne did all the work. I couldn't even play with Taylor and Griffin. What was my life becoming? Time was dragging on. Finally the day came and the procedure was uncomfortable. I had to lie on my stomach and let my breast hang in a hole that was isolated. Horrible.

A few days later I met with the bearers of *bad* news. Two women sat down with me in a small room and described the severity of my situation. I had stage II breast cancer. Not good. After a heart-to-heart with Dr. Sharon, surgery was scheduled. Judge Jill made a special trip to Colorado Springs to be with me for the surgery. It was outpatient surgery for a mastectomy. Outpatient! Go figure. Now time was flying. My breast was going to be removed in a matter of moments. Jillie and Page were there when they took me away on the gurney. Everyone was very sweet to me, and then I drifted away.

Ingrid's face was up close to me as I was coming out, and she said, "Ginny, all three of the lymph nodes in your nipple were malignant, so I had to take eighteen more from under your arm. The tests will be back in two days, and I will call you with the results." My brother Matt was waiting for me with Page after the surgery. Matt and Ara volunteered to take care of me after the surgery. I wouldn't be able to drive for three weeks. Thank the universe for Ara. She was another angel in my life. The recuperation from breast removal was brutal. Rubber drainage tubes came out of both sides of my chest cavity. They had to be emptied every four hours. Taking a shower was painful. My skin hurt. Ara got right in the shower with me and washed my entire body and my hair. I felt so grateful for her love. She was a very special friend, more like a sister really.

Ingrid called me in the evening. She was very sorry to have to tell me that twelve of the lymph nodes were positive. I definitely should have chemotherapy, and I needed to have a PET scan. I wasn't sure I could do the chemo. I had to think about it. Why did I really want to fight cancer only to come back to what seemed to be progressive MS? The chemo might kill me because of the MS. After the PET scan I met with the oncologist who was assigned to me, Dr. Hoyer. He had a limp handshake. My bother was present in the room when he told me the cancer was in my liver and a lymph node under my collarbone that was inoperable. I had stage IV breast cancer that had metastasized in my liver. I should have a liver biopsy to confirm the location. The liver cannot be radiated, so there would be no radiation. It was a death sentence. I should start the chemotherapy right away. "Could I wait until after Christine's wedding because my grandchildren are going to be flower girl and ring bearer? It is only another ten days. It's their aunt's wedding—Chas's sister."

My chemotherapy started at the end of December. I didn't get out of bed for the whole week before. I was terrified. I cried, and Dewayne cried with me. He told me he would never leave me as long as I was sick. We called Sanaviv in Mexico to see if there were alternative treatments. It was cost-prohibitive, and they didn't really have anything better to offer. Cancer is cancer. Chemotherapy is the best treatment available. Alternative therapy isn't the best way to fight cancer. The day finally came and a friend drove me to the treatment center at Memorial. I wore a scarf and fleece hat because my hair looked sickly like me. I felt so unattractive, and I tried to hide my face. I had lost most of my self-esteem, and I was very depressed. Dr. Hoyer had started me on Effexor. The oncology nurses saved me. They were guardian angels in disguise. I loved every one of them, and they loved me back.

Looking back, that first treatment wasn't bad at all. I had been loaded up with expensive antinausea drugs and medicine to help with diarrhea. I actually had to go to a two-hour-long class on how to take care of myself during chemotherapy. I was instructed on how to take care of sores in my mouth, dry skin, hair loss, nausea, loss of appetite, fingernails and toenails falling off or turning black, and neuropathy. Most of that never happened to me except the loss of appetite and hair. I already had lived with neuropathy from the MS for several years, so I was okay with that. It wasn't fun, but I could live with it. I asked to bump up the Effexor because I wanted to find a way to be more positive. I knew that was crucial in healing. Each week I seemed to handle everything a little better. Dewayne made sure I was eating. He cooked for me and took me out to dinner. He juiced for me on a regular basis. He spent a small fortune on organic fruits and vegetables. He loaded me up with vitamins, but not too many antioxidants because the doctors said they could hinder the effectiveness of the chemo.

I figured out pretty quickly that the pretreatment was my favorite part of the chemo regimen. Every Monday for sixteen weeks I got warm blankets; benedryl, which made me pleasantly sleepy; pepcid, which settled my stomach; and a giant dose of *steroid* through the IV. Dr. Hoyer told me it was a hundred times more powerful than oral steroids. By week seven, I was loving chemotherapy. Three days after Hoyer upped my dose of Effexor for a third time, I woke up at Dewayne's and felt *happy*! It was incredible! My friend, Barbara Stanley, had given me her wig, and I looked beautiful in it. I started wearing full eye makeup and dressing in some of my beautiful clothes. It was fun to go to chemo and wow the nurses with my newfound style. I told them I loved chemo, and they were all amazed. I felt happy, and the steroids took all my pain away for four days. Happy and no pain, now that's a winning combination. Every time my blood work was close to perfect. I never had to miss a chemo treatment as a lot of folks did. I would see people leave crying or frustrated because their blood work wasn't good enough to tolerate the chemo. Things were going so well that I planned to go on my yearly trip to Scottsdale to see my three sister friends. By the time I went, I only had one treatment left after I got back. It was fun to feel so good and be with my friends laughing and partying like old times. They all spoiled me as usual. We went to see a Dale Chihuly installation at the Botanical Gardens on a beautiful, magical night in the Arizona desert. I went home to Colorado completely refreshed and energized and ready for my last treatment. On April 1 I had a PET scan. I knew it was April Fool's Day, but that didn't matter at all. They injected me with radioactive sugar water and shoved me into the machine for twenty-five minutes. I looked up at the blue-sky tile on the ceiling and prayed for the most benevolent outcome just like Meggie told me to do. I was asleep when it was finished.

Remission

April 3, 2009, will forever be burned in my memory as one of the most significant days of my life. I started out in the morning with my new ritual of getting into my red Little Giraffe robe that I had special ordered from Mountain Moppets before I sold it because it was the most luxurious fabric I knew of, soft and plush. I turned on my new teapot, which Dewayne bought me just because I said I loved it, took my favorite mug out of the cupboard, the one Basia had given me years ago with a hand-painted sunflower on it like a kid would draw, threw a green tea bag in it, and waited for the water to boil and the whistle to start singing. When the tea was ready, I poured it, added some almond milk and a teaspoon of Xylitol, and then took my usual place on my love seat and turned on *Good Morning America.* I like to multitask, so I started looking at my bills. I knew I had to be at my oncology doctor's office at ten thirty, and I really didn't want to be late for this one because it was a very important appointment. I was going to find out the results of my PET scan. I remembered to take my antidepressant, which I take religiously every morning without fail. It has saved my life, so I never forget. I noticed that on the side of my mortgage statement it said I could refinance my house with no closing costs or fees and get a better rate. The recession has been good for some of us in some ways. However, my eldest brother had most of his retirement income invested with Bernie Maddoff for the last eighteen years, and he never touched it, so he got screwed in more ways than you can imagine. I think it has taken its toll on him and his family.

Anyway, I called the bank because I thought I would have enough time before the doctor's appointment, but I was wrong because the representative wanted to do the whole refinance over the phone, so I hung in there because it was going to save me more than $100 a month. When we were finally finished, I had like twenty minutes to put on all my makeup and the most beautiful wig a friend just gave me because she had breast cancer twelve years ago and figured she wouldn't need it. I admire this girl tremendously because she married a guy who used to be in a really cool band, and he got Lou Gehrig's disease. He lived for a long time, years, he beat the odds there, but when he finally died, she was devastated. They were really in love those two. I ran back to the bathroom and did my best job of multitasking—putting on my eyes, which are my best feature, flossing and brushing my teeth, then doing all my skin care that saved my skin during chemotherapy, which normally destroys people's skin. I was religious about it morning and night because it is all botanicals with no mineral oil. My skin looks beautiful for a gal who is almost sixty. Then I applied the final touch of lipstick and gloss. Damn, my eyes were runny from the taxetere, which is the toxic part of the chemotherapy. Tears are really one of the best detoxifiers our body has. You should always let yourself cry because whatever emotion you are feeling, the tears release the cortisol from your body. Cortisol is the flight or fight hormone that can do tremendous harm to your body if you don't let it out.

So okay, now I'm ready except for my vitamins and supplements, so I grab them with a mug of energy drink with all the vitamin Bs, which are extremely important to heal my MS.

I drive my trusty 2001 Lexus to the doctor's as fast as I can without putting myself in danger because now I really want to live. I still see by the clock in my car that I'm going to be a half hour late, which is totally unacceptable. What can I do now but just continue on and not worry because I am totally past worrying anymore about anything. I've been asking a lot of people that I meet over ninety what their secret is, and they all say, "I've never been a big worrier." Up until about a month ago I have been a big worrier. Today I'm not worrying about anything, not even the doctor's appointment because I already know what they are going to tell me.

I park my car and remember to put the yellow sign in my window that says Oncology Outpatient. Off I go without my cane because I feel and look so damn good, up the escalator and into the office with a big beautiful smile on my face. The receptionist gives me a big smile and tells me how great I look. Then I start apologizing for my tardiness, and she just ignores that and says the doctor will see me in a few moments. I look across the reception room, and there is my oncology doctor who has a limp handshake and doesn't seem that comfortable in his own skin, but he is brilliant, and I just love him. He is looking down at someone's chart and then he looks up, sees me, and then flashes this *huge* smile at me. "Hi, Dr. Hoyer!"

Then the nurse comes who is just a doll, and she wants to weigh me and take my vitals all the while telling me how great I look and asks how I have been doing. She has no idea how happy I am feeling, that I am really in a state of euphoria where I want to hug everybody. That must be what the drug ecstasy feels like according to my daughter and a few others I know who have tried it. We spend the next few minutes talking about decorating our houses. It turns out we both love black and red and leopard print together. That is exactly how my house is decorated. She asked me to bring pictures next time. Then Dr. John enters the room. He is a physician assistant, and he is tall and handsome. He seats himself across from me with his file. He tells me how amazing I look and asks how I'm feeling and I say, "Just great." "Well, I have your file here with results of your PET scan." I was very calm. "We expected good results, but not these results. It says here that there isn't one cancer cell in your body. You are 100 percent cancer-free. You are in *remission!*" Well, I just stared at him for a couple of seconds; then I came out of my chair, and we hugged each other. I felt so comfortable in his arms. I wasn't really crying, just on the verge. Then Dr. Hoyer knocked on the door and came in. This humble man saved my life by the thoughtful protocol he put me on with chemotherapy. I had chemo every Monday for sixteen weeks. Three weeks with both Taxatere and Herceptin and then one week of just

Herceptin. Taxatere is the toxic one and Herceptin is a biological drug that is specific to the kind of cancer I had, HR2-positive. I'm lucky that this is the kind of breast cancer I had. Herceptin is a new drug; it's only been around for about five years. It is the most technologically advanced cancer drug thus far, and it costs a shocking $10,000 per treatment. I absolutely loved chemotherapy; weird, huh? Nobody says that, but it was true. The reason why I loved it was because of the premeds they give you to alleviate some of the endless nasty side effects of the highly toxic and powerful cancer medication. They feed it to you through what they call a port that has to be surgically implanted to access a large vein in one's chest. The smaller veins in the arm or wrist could not handle the toxicity.

Here is a funny story. I was at my Monday morning chemo session, which takes anywhere from four to six hours unless something bad happens. Here's how it goes. First you get your premeds. One bag of Dexedrine, the steroid I love, love, love, but not right away. Then comes the benedryl, which really starts to slow me down. I'm usually talking to the person next to me, and no matter who they are, I find them very interesting by asking them enough questions to learn what is special about them. When the benedryl starts kicking in, I become very sleepy, and I try to get the attention of one of the nurses or volunteers who are really angels in disguise to bring me a blanket that has been specially warmed in some kind of a machine. They bring it to me and lovingly cover my long body. It's a very womblike feeling, and I generally drift right off into a very peaceful sleep. Suddenly I am awake because I really have to go to the bathroom. I don't have a lot of time because when I have to go, I have to go *now*. First you have to unplug the IV machine, then push the pole with you to the bathroom and close the extremely heavy door shut. Oh, thank you, relief is here. So I sit down to pee, and right away I notice there is a pool of water under the pole. What is that? Oh my god, there is a red tube hanging and dripping on the floor. What happened? I knew I had to tell the nurse, so I picked up the tube that was dripping on the floor, put it up on the machine so it would stop leaking, and headed out of the bathroom to go back to my lounge chair. I was just about to get the attention of a nurse/angel when the nurse helping a patient near me looked over and dropped everything she was doing. On came the paper booties and gloves and paper coats, and she yelled at me to wash my hands with disinfectant quickly. The *hazmat* team showed up almost immediately, and everything had to be done in proper order. There was lots of chaos, and I just sat there staring at the guy across from me. We both started laughing so hard because we both knew that this unbelievably toxic material was going directly into our veins. All the angels started calling me a troublemaker, and we all had to stay late because they actually replaced the exact amount of chemo that I lost and all the angels had to fill out special paperwork about the incident. It was determined that the red rubber hose was defective and that all materials involved had to go into a bright yellow *hazmat* bag for disposal in the toxic waste area of the hospital. I lovingly became known as the troublemaker. So I practically attacked Dr. Hoyer with my gushing little girl voice telling how grateful I was that he saved my life and gave me a window into knowing how I could cure my MS. He kept smiling and began backing out of the room saying he needed to see the other patients. I think he was trying not to cry.

Dr. John and I sat back down, and I asked him when I could get my silicone implant finished; he said I could go for it in one more week. I told him I wasn't going to get a nipple tattooed on it; I was going to get a sunflower with the stem and leaf tattooed there so it could cover up my scar. He loved that idea and made some creative suggestions. Then he said to look behind me, and right there on the wall behind my head was a photograph of a field of sunflowers.

Then it was time to leave the office, so I hugged him again, and I felt so small in his arms even though I am 5'10". When I walked out of the room, everyone started to hug me and congratulate me. I heard someone in the waiting room say, "Is that Ginny?" It was my fellow chemo friend, Lou, and she said, "I would know that voice anywhere." I made my next appointment. From that moment on I was in a state of euphoria, and I've been there ever since. My daughter, Page, has even said to me, "Mom, do you think maybe you should call the doctor and see if you should maybe ramp back on your antidepressant because you're kind of manic, you know?"

I had already planned a celebration party—kind of gutsy of me, but I really knew with great certainty that I was cancer-free way before my appointment. I invited Dewayne, my brother Matt and his family, Michael, Page and Chas, and of course, my grandbabies, Taylor and Griffin. We all met at Trinity Brewery on Garden of the Gods Road. It was a fun place to have a family gathering because of the sofas in the back area and the way they could be arranged to accommodate that many people. When Matt arrived, he immediately took orders for beer and went to the bar to get them for everyone. All the beers at Trinity have names. When he came back with the brews, I asked him what the name was. Arrogant bastard was his reply. I cracked up because that is really what he is at times. Everyone else was amused as well. I was so happy to have these very important people in my life surrounding me. It was a total love fest that night for my miracle and me. I am a very lucky girl and feel so grateful for my healing. What an incredible group of people my family is. We were all celebrating together. It was just the best.

After that evening, I set out calling all my very special people who live in other parts of the country. I called Mark Tierney in Playa del Carmen, Mexico. I called Meggie in Scottsdale, Kimmie Patty, Jillie, and my brother Tom and his wife, Diane, in Minneapolis. Everyone had the same reaction. Complete jubilation. How wonderful to be able to deliver that joyous news to everyone. At that point I started letting the reality sink in. I am a Miracle Girl, *wow*.

This is the point I started getting serious about planning a reunion of my college friends, a special group of four guys and two girls. I was one of the girls and the other is my lifelong friend, Jillie, who is now a judge on the second district court of appeals in St. Paul, Minnesota. I started the ball rolling by calling my friend, Dean, who I have actually stayed in touch with over the forty years since we were all together at the University of Colorado at Boulder. He put together the contact list of all the guys. In addition he included a PS at the end of the e-mail that said the following: Someone said we should invite Noble Irving to come because he would enjoy seeing everyone. I can't believe I am actually seeing that name, Noble Irving, on the Internet.

Noble

Right now I feel like I'm in a supereuphoric state because I've been waiting for Noble to arrive at my house after a long drive from Naples, Florida. I feel like I am being teased, so the sex will be superexciting. I haven't seen him in thirty-five years, and I know I will not be disappointed because a friend who has spent quite a bit of time with him said he has aged very well. I was worried he might be bald because he was so blond when I last saw him thirty-five years ago, but Chris said he's not bald at all. It's ironic and really funny because I'm the one who is bald from the sixteen weeks of chemo, but I look really good because I spent a fair amount of time on skin care, and the wig that Barbara gave me is awesome. No one knows it's a wig unless I decide to tell them. I'm not sure how good I look without makeup and the hair, but my skin is beautiful, and you know what they say, "Beauty is in the eye of the beholder." Noble is my dream come true of the perfect man and the perfect lover. I'm sure he is like fine wine. The older it gets, the better. He should be here late tonight depending if he has one of those things in his car that detects cops, a fuzz-buster. He is very responsible and respectful of people who deserve respect. I have been shopping a lot because it makes me happy to buy gifts for people and myself if I love it so much and it's on sale. Sometimes I will pay full price if I think something will bring someone pleasure like Kamasutra oil, which can be licked off because it is chocolate mint of aphrodisiac oils to rub on your skin in all the right places. I wonder what will happen when he first pulls up in my driveway and we see each other for the first time in thirty-five years. This is the most amazing miracle. I have miracles every day now. Sometimes they come right away after I first think about what I want to happen, and with Noble it took thirty-five years of thinking about him. I know why it took that long. I had to get Mike and Dewayne out of my head, but especially Mike. When that happened, then the universe found a way to get us together. I know for sure now that "what you think about you bring about"—the law of attraction and the power of positive thinking. That's the secret of the universe.

I'm in a state of euphoria now, but I'm sure when Noble gets here, I will be in Nirvana. We are going to Beijing, China, for three months together in a few weeks. I have received a number of different reactions from friends and family. They range from, "Ginny, you are living a dream and a miracle," to "Ginny, are you crazy? Come on now. It does seem like a fairy tale."

I'm lying on the love seat, listening to my favorite selection of music on iTunes. The Prize called me about an hour ago and said he was in Limon, Colorado. He made excellent time because he has a tremendous ability to focus on the moment. I am learning that living in the moment encompasses his current philosophy of life. I'm a little different in that I have learned to live in the moment, but I have to add hope to the equation because that was how I healed myself from cancer along with the chemotherapy and the Herceptin and the collective prayers of many, many people who love me and I love them back. I believe collective prayer, no matter what your religious or spiritual belief system, is very powerful. My friend Meggie turned me on to that concept way back in the beginning after my mastectomy when things were going from bad to worse. I have left the garage door and the front door open so he can pull right in and walk right in. Clever of me.

All of a sudden I hear a rumbling sound in the garage, like he's here and he's revving the engine of the mystery car. Oh god, it's eleven thirty and he's finally here. I sit up and wait for him to come in. It sounds like he is taking things out of the car. It seems like a long time before the door opens and then he says my name and peeks in. Is that him? He used to be a lot more blond, almost like a towhead, and his hair was curly, like an Adonis, but not too curly, just perfect. I stare at him. Then he walks past me and looks at me and says he needs a shower. Oh, okay, I can deal with that. I wouldn't want to hug anyone if I had just driven for two straight days and nights with very little sleep and when you did sleep it was on a sheet of bubble wrap and two pillows from Goodwill. Incidentally,

I love both the pillows and will keep them; one is black with a beautiful needlepoint of two strappy bright red 5" high heels on a white background. The other one is black with a very cool zebra heavy fabric on top and a very small split in the seam, which I can easily fix. They give me a whole new appreciation of Goodwill, where The Prize buys most of his clothes, as I learn soon enough. Of course, he will never get those pillows back. I'm keeping 'em.

So I tell him to go on back to the shower in the room with the king-sized bed and the king-sized bathroom, and help himself to the orange towels that I washed with Downey fabric softener, to make them soft and smell good. I have this adorable little house that I have loved decorating in my own unique style of red, black, earth tones, and leopard print accents. The rug in my cozy little living room has zebra print in the middle and leopard print around the edges in earth tones and black. So classy. While Noble is in the bathroom, I go out the garage to see what his car is. What a shocker! It is a royal blue Toyota M3 with a kit and all this silver writing on it like race car drivers have; it's a convertible with a black top and black leather bucket seats. I feel like I'm a twenty-five-year-old again. Jesus.

Pretty soon he comes back into the living room. Now he has shorts and a T-shirt on. He's bigger than I remember. He was really a twenty-five-year-old boy when I last saw him, and now he is a sixty-year-old man. He is very, very handsome. He was beautiful then, a beautiful blond boy with curly hair. I remember exactly what he looked like and exactly what he said to me the last time we were together.

We were driving home from northern Wisconsin where we went to a cabin with two couples who were good friends of Mike's and mine for a lot of years. Noble was driving my new bright yellow 1972 Volkswagen bug with a black racing stripe. I was a flight attendant for Northwest Airlines at that time and was making good money. I'm pretty sure gas was twenty-five cents a gallon. I started telling him that I really liked him and asked when we could see each other again, and he stopped me. He said, "I think you should go back to Mike. I know he really loves you. You're the kind of girl that needs to be deeply loved, and I can't do that right now. I have some problems. You can't fix them." Even though we didn't hear that much about depression back then, I knew what he meant. So I let him go back then.

Now he's in my living room, and I tell him to come and sit next to me on the love seat. He comes around the coffee table, sits down, and puts his hand on my knee. I lean over and kiss him. I want more, and he says, "We're not going to do this now. I need to go to bed. I'm so tired." So we talked for a little while, and I asked him why he never married. Did he want kids? He said yes, but he was afraid he might pass the depression factor along. There were two girls he would have married and had babies with, but neither one worked out. He said he would have had babies with me, for sure. That was a pretty sexy thing to say. I can feel the raw sexual attraction we had when we were young. For me, it is palpable. Now he wants to go to bed. What? I've got adrenaline coursing through my veins, and he wants to go to bed? By himself. Keep your cool, Ginny; let him go to bed, I say to myself. He's been driving straight for two days and two nights just to get to me faster. Give him a break. He goes to the king-sized bed and leaves me alone on the sofa. Almost immediately I hear him lightly snoring.

It takes me a while to calm down. I just sit there, going over everything in my head. Finally, I get up and go through his bedroom to my bathroom where all my skin care is, and also the makeshift wig stand, which is a champagne decorative tin container that came with the wig. My friend, Barbara Stanley, gave it to me, because she figured she didn't need it anymore. She is a breast cancer survivor deluxe and a person I greatly admire. She was married for many years to the love of her life, Chris, of Flash Cadillac fame, the Colorado Springs-based rock band. He suffered from Lou Gehrig's disease for so many years. No one could believe he could live that long. I think it was because he loved her so much. She loved him just as much and always tried to make his life a joy. I think they had a pact about his dying. He's gone now, and she is trying hard to pick up her life. It's been rough for her, but she's a strong one. I just adore her.

I do my skin care routine religiously because it saved my skin from the ravages of chemotherapy. Then I put on my jammies and try to sneak through the room silently. Noble speaks up and says not to worry about him, just do what I need to do. I tell him to come into my room in the morning. I go to my room and take a Xanax to calm my nerves. Then I crawl into my womblike bed and finally drop into a deep sleep.

The sweetest thing wakes me up in the morning. Noble is there around on the side of the bed I don't sleep on, and he is crawling into the bed with me and then wrapping his arms around me like I'm a little girl. I think we may have kissed, but we just started talking right away, and I think the tears started flowing with me as they always do. I just let it all pour out. He wants to know all about my life, and when I try to recount it, the tragedies just go on and on, and I can't believe it myself how much I have gone through. I think he interjected a few things about his life over the past thirty-five years, but mostly it was about me. We talked for a couple of hours.

I want to make love with him, so I pull out some Kamasutra oil, which I have never used in my life, but I bought especially for him just for fun. It was chocolate flavored. I ask him if he wants to try it on me or whether I should try it on him. He says I could try it on him. Okay, I love that idea, so I pour some on his chest, actually too much. I start licking it off his chest, and it tastes good, but there's too much, and then Noble says, "I don't really need that stuff to be turned on by you." Quickly this lovemaking becomes about my pleasure and me. This is just exquisite for me, and he is that sexy and giving person I remember him being all those years ago. I'm satisfied and I'm hungry, and so is he. We decide to make some breakfast; only I end up making breakfast because he wants to get his computer set up. He is all about getting our visas for China. How exciting is this? He comes in the kitchen and tells me he needs to speak to my oncology doctor about going for three months. He thinks it's probably too long. I think so too because I want to spend most of the summer in Colorado.

I cook the breakfast, and after a while we decide to go for a ride in the chick magnet car. I feel so happy riding next to him in this totally sexy car. We go to the health food store two blocks from my house, Mountain Mama's, to pick a supplement for my nerve pain that actually has Chinese herbs in it. Noble runs in to get it, and while he's in there a couple of thirty-something girls are walking toward the car from across the parking lot. Noble comes out of the store and starts to get in the car. The girls start whistling at him with me sitting right there. As they pass the car, I say, "Isn't he gorgeous?" What a trip! When he gets in the car, he turns to me and says, "This happens all the time." Like it's no big deal. What a sexy, unaffected man. I really do love him. We spend the rest of the day playing. We stop at Mountain Moppets to check out the shop I used to own. Noble needs a gift for baby Justin who is his eighteen-month-old Chinese/Taiwanese godchild. He picks a baseball cap that says *Colorado* and a pair of Robeez leather baby shoes that have a race car on them. Cute.

Justin comes from the gene pool of Jason and Sandra. Jason thinks his son will be the first Chinese president of the United States. Noble met Jason when they both shared a workspace while they were electrical engineers together in Seattle. They worked together for seven years. They are best friends. Noble was the best man in his wedding when he married Sandra. Jason moved back to China when his dad became sick. Apparently it was a debacle, and Jason became upset with his healthcare in China. I think he had a heart problem. His father died, and Jason's mom lives in Shanghai alone now. Jason's mom designed the entire subway system in Shanghai, and his father designed the entire hydroelectric system in China. *Wow!* I think Jason's right about his son.

Now we head on down to The Loop, my brother Matt's super successful Mexican restaurant in Manitou Springs. I'm pretty sure that restaurant has made him a millionaire. He has his own plane. He seems to be on top of the world with his beautiful Mexican wife, Ara. She is really spectacular looking in an exotic way, and she's one of my best friends. She got in the shower with me when I was recovering from my mastectomy and was so depressed. She would wash me, then dry me off and put lotion all over my body because my skin was so dry. She would spend an hour drying my hair and curling it with hot rollers. I remember looking at myself and feeling so sad and unattractive with my gray hair. Going gray was a bad mistake. I told her how much I loved her, and we both cried. She said she just wanted to treat me as if I were her own mother. I really love Ara; she's one of my people. She is twenty-four years younger than my brother. They have a son, Gustavo, who Ara came into the marriage with. He is fourteen years old and will be a lady-killer. He already kills me; he is so incredibly handsome. He is also a complete gentleman, thanks to Ara's mothering skills. Then there is Nikki, my only niece, and she is a beauty. We all think she has my eyes because they are huge and no one in Ara's family has big eyes. Nikki is twelve and tall and very slender like Page and me. She has the most beautiful skin I have ever seen. She is very special and talented. She has a beautiful voice, and we think it might come from her grandmother, my mother and of course, Matt's mother. She sang opera style when she was a young woman.

Noble and I had a margarita, which has won "Best of the Springs" in the *Gazette* and *Independent* many times. Then we had some great Mexican food thanks to Heron, the amazing chef that has been with Matt as long as he has owned the restaurant. After lunch I think we went to mi casa to have a nap. Noble and I came to love our naps. We always took our naps in separate bedrooms so we could really sleep. Life was like a fairytale for that week. He stayed for a whole week. I didn't expect that. It was so relaxing to be with him. He just wanted to make me happy. He would say, "You've been through a lot, Ginny." Then he would tell me I have a beautiful face and he liked my body type—long legs and tall and slim. He said a lot of nice things to me and made me feel special every day. We always did what I wanted. My dear friend Wendy Nelson of Blue Fox Photography offered to do a photo shoot of the two of us for free. That was a lot of fun, and I knew I would use her photos for this book. As far as I'm concerned, she's the best photographer I have ever known. She has made my family famous, even my daughter and son-in-law's dog, Blue. She has photographed my grandchildren and Page and Chas a number of times. She did the most fabulous photos for Mountain Moppets for years and years.

We have been like partners in business. My business benefited hers and hers benefited mine.

Noble and I went to Goodwill to shop for him; he likes it there. I've never shopped there in my life, so it was a new adventure for me. I was amazed; we found a Perry Ellis shirt that was actually pressed, and another really nice blue plaid shirt. Noble looks fabulous in blue because he has huge blue eyes and he is very handsome. I wish he were a little taller. He's not as tall as I am; I'm 5'10" or maybe 11".

Our photo shoot was awesome, sexy, and fun. I love those pictures that resulted from that shoot. There were a couple of red flags though. We were going to meet my brother Matt at the Broadmoor for dinner, and on the way Noble yelled loud at me in the car. It was something about how I really had a thing about money because I had commented on how I would love to find a blue cashmere sweater for him because it was chilly that night. He really raised his voice, and I was shocked. I tried to diffuse it by just not reacting. After about three blocks we stopped at a stop sign, and he turned to me and said, "I may have overreacted about the sweater thing. I'm sorry." I was relieved he said that because that really did shock me. Dinner was lovely at The Summit. We created quite a stir when we pulled up in that fast and furious car. I think it was prom night and there were quite a few kids, all dressed up and having fun. It was pretty cool getting out of the car and having all eyes on both of us. Noble didn't valet the car; instead he pulled it out and parked it underground.

Courtesy of *www.bluefoxphotography.com*

Matt met me inside, and we ordered a drink while we waited for Noble to come up. We were seated right away and just settled in to have a great dinner. I seem to always feel like a princess with two good-looking men wanting to show me a good time while having a good time themselves. Matt seemed to be pretty interested in Noble because he said he'd had his pilot's license for twenty years. Matt has had his pilot's license for about two years. I have flown once with Matt when I was recovering from my breast surgery. I was still very depressed, but it was a good diversion at a time when I really needed it. Matt has been an excellent brother to me most of my life, but I have been a better sister to him. He can be a real bastard to me and Ara too. Thankfully he comes through when I really need him.

Noble picked up the bill for the entire evening, which was very gracious of him because Matt wanted to pick up the tab. It's apparent Noble has been raised with a lot of class. He never talks about himself unless you ask him a question, then he talks quite a bit.

We had one other big disagreement that caused quite a few tears and an actual fight between us, but we were able to resolve it for a time. I figured out after many conversations that Noble never told anyone about me. No one. That upset me a little because I told everyone about him. Different styles, I guess, but it made me feel a little invisible, so I called him on it. He saw how upset it made me, so he promised he would talk about me to people of importance, like his mother. Noble has a policy with his ninety-year-old mother of don't ask, don't tell. He doesn't want her to know about his sexual escapades, because she might judge him. That is intolerable to him. I think he's wrong about that, but what do I really know about that. That's his business and hers. Enough said. He did tell me his mother knew I was going to China with him. Also his sister, Marcia, knows about me. I don't think anyone else knows about me except his friend, Mark, in Seattle and Manh. Oh, that Manh is something else. What an amazing miracle he is. Manh is Cambodian, and he had quite a story to tell me when I finally arrived in Seattle. I fell in love with Manh only a few days after I met him. He is one perfect human being. He really treated me like precious cargo while I was in Seattle before leaving for Beijing. I couldn't help myself; he was just too perfect and hilariously funny and tender and understanding and just so totally cool. I could spend the rest of my life with him. Next to Noble, he was a firecracker, just like me really. We just fit together like Harold and Maude! Oh, how I loved to be with that twenty-seven-year-old man.

This story is getting a little bit tedious about Noble, so I want to get on to Manh. I will finish up Noble's visit with his leaving and driving back to Seattle and then a wait of about ten days when I attended my goddaughter Emma's graduation in Boulder, which was a magnificent affair. Noble and I skyped during the wait, and things began to slowly deteriorate. He made the giant mistake of seeing his psychiatrist for *add* medication because he wanted to learn Chinese on his sixth visit to China. This is a man he has seen for twenty-five years. Who sees the same shrink for twenty-five years except for Woody Allen? If they don't help you after a few years, move on. Noble hadn't seen the guy for a couple of years, I guess, but he really did a number on Noble this time. Our conversations went from, "I feel kind of negative about our relationship" to "You're kind of like a stalker, Ginny." I was blindsided, and like the good little girl that I am, I persevered like I always have with every man I've ever been with. It was too late; the tickets to Beijing were paid for, and our visas had arrived. What Noble did to me was a Dr. Jekyll and Mr. Hyde. I was caught in a whirlwind that I would learn was completely out of my control.

Manh

Manh saved me, like my symbol, Mark Tierney. He took a situation that was becoming a catastrophe and made it magical. Manh has a unique way of looking at the world. He taught me one of the most valuable tools to survive anything life throws at you. When someone you love more than yourself (like your daughter or grandchildren) dies, you just have to know they die only when they are perfect and thus ready to move on to a more beautiful place than this world we live in. Just that easy to accept tragedy. It changed everything for me. I know I can handle anything in my life now because of what Manh told me. He's making a custom football helmet for my grandson for his third birthday with the Denver Broncos decal on it. Very cool. He is going to make a giant custom transformer for Griffin's third birthday as well. I watched him paint one before things got totally crazy after I got back to Seattle from Beijing.

I'm sitting in Denver Airport waiting for my plane to Seattle. As usual, I have made many, many new friends. I've handed out a few business cards and told numerous people about some of my miracles, and it's fun to see the expressions on their faces when I tell them the fairy tale about Noble and me. Women are incurable romantics, and I can peak their interest by telling them that he is my lover and that we hadn't seen each other in three-five years.

I swear I would not even have recognized Noble on the street; he had changed so much. I think I look almost exactly the same as I did back then, only with a few wrinkles, but same face and same body. He, on the other hand, looks totally different. He is still very handsome, but a totally different face and body. However, that smile just brings back all the memories of youth and lust. His voice is still the same, and the sound of it just intoxicates me. He has no idea the effect he has on me. I want him to worship me like he did, but it could never be that easy. My friend, Mark, warned me to go slow. He understands how men think. Totally different than women. Life seems totally clear to me and my feelings for him. He seems to be holding back, and I have no idea why. He's more complicated than most men I know. He knows how he wants things to be, and when I say something that triggers his anger, he can just lose it. It shocks me because I don't think of him as losing control, but he does, and then I have to be very measured in how I choose my words.

He has only e-mailed me for the past few days. No phone calls. Give it time. I really can't remember the flight from Denver to Seattle. He called me when we were on the ground. I had a wheelchair waiting for me when I got off the plane. A girl wheeled me to the waiting area where Noble was waiting for me. When I got up from the wheelchair, I walked to him and tried to grab a kiss, but it was not good. We went straight to his friend Mark's house, who wasn't even there. He's been in Las Vegas for a few months. It was late night, maybe about twelve thirty.

Waiting for us with a smile and conversation was Manh, a Cambodian boy/man who I learned was twenty-seven. Another miracle was happening. Manh started talking a lot—kind of like Ginny on steroids. I learned so much about him fast. He was a very interesting guy. He was born in Cambodia. He and his mother, father, and brother came to the United States, but the Vietnamese executed most of the rest of his family. That must have been the Khmer Rouge. Heartbreaking. But this guy had confidence. He designed furniture, had a great education, and was in business with Mark, the guy who owned this house. He was very sweet to make our bed and light candles so it would smell good and be inviting, which it was. The bed was quite beautiful with a green silk bedspread and decorative pillows, designer style. This was Mark's bed.

I had a glass of wine, and Manh and I talked for a few hours about many different subjects, the last one being the possibility of the end of civilization in 2012. I had been thinking it might possibly happen because the Inca, Aztec, and Mayan calendars end then. The Bible talks about it, and so did Nostradamus. Manh said he was a little freaked out about it, but I'm not. Noble hardly said a word the whole time. He did say he was tired and had to go to bed, and so was I; so that is what we did. I had to lie right next to Noble because I was cold. He was so warm in bed, like a furnace, as I like to say. He let me snuggle in close to him. I did sleep well after a while. Many thoughts were going through my brain at this point. Many feelings and emotions were going through my body. I felt starved for affection. Noble wouldn't kiss me in the car when I asked him to. He said he wasn't going to do any kissing then. I don't get it; what does kissing mean to him? I felt stung when he said that, but I tucked it away, like a *good girl*. I want him to put his arms around me and hug me.

I snuggled next to him until about seven the next morning; then he was up and wanted out of there. What did I want for breakfast? Oatmeal, blueberries, and almond milk. He went out and bought exactly what I wanted. Then he was gone. He left to work on his house. He's been working on it for the ten days before I came. Will he ever be done and have time for me? Call him when I wake up. He doesn't like to talk on the phone, but he does it because he knows I like it. Most of the time I feel a little sting, but I'm getting used to it. I've had the thought that maybe he won't give me what I need either because he can't or, worse, maybe he doesn't want to. He is very complicated. What has his life really been like with the depression? He has explained a lot to me about coping with his depression and why he seems a little flat at times. I went back to sleep until about ten, and when I opened my eyes, I was looking at an amazing giant papier-mâché smiling jester head with really big lips. It was attached to a beam running across the ceiling. I loved it, but I remember Manh said it creeped him out when he took us to the candlelit room last night. It was fun art, so I took a few pictures of it during one of my visits there. I got out of bed and went out to the living room to see if I could set my computer up and get the iTunes going. I love to wake up to music, my music. I played it as loud as it would go, and then I called Noble.

"Listen, I need to work on my house today, so Manh will take you downtown with him so you can see the EMP—Experience Music Project." "Okay, but he's still sleeping." "Well, go knock on his door and wake him up." I knocked on Manh's door, and he came all tousled black hair, looking like he hardly knew who I was and where he was. I handed him the phone so Noble could talk to him. They talked; then Manh handed me the phone, and Noble told me Manh would take really good care of me and give me a really good time. That was a huge understatement! I was about to go on a magical mystery tour with an almost perfect person. I'm not kidding.

Manh told me to get ready, so I picked out some clothes and headed to the bathroom. First I washed my face and did my whole skin care routine, which was now Lluvia from the Amazon Rain forest. It's the best I've ever used because of the quality of the ingredients. It is from Olivia Newton-John and her husband John's company, Amazon Herb. It has many extraordinary products that are made from the rich nutrients in the rain forest. They give a portion of the proceeds back to the indigenous of the forest. I love that because we all need to be concerned about the destruction of the rain forest. If we lose the rain forest we will not survive as the human race. It's one of my personal causes. I continued with my make-up and my beautiful wig that fools all the people and felt totally gorgeous when we went out to downtown Seattle big-time.

Manh is a totally cool guy with all the perfect clothes, shoes, sunglasses, and iPhone. He was very articulate and extremely witty and funny. He was the most amazing match for me because we just got each other. There was smooth flowing conversation all the time. I was totally comfortable with him and felt safe. He was a real gentlemen—a Renaissance man who treated everyone with respect, especially women. I was about to find out how fun loving he really was.

We left the house and drove to the Park and Ride in Mark's SUV and then waited just a few minutes and got on the bus. Seattle has an unbelievable transportation system, which everyone seems to take advantage of. After I was comfortably seated, I started really observing what was around me. What a spectacular city! In Colorado Springs one's eye focuses up to the beautiful Rocky Mountains and Pike's Peak, but in Seattle one's eye focuses at sea level where everything is in Technicolor—green grass and trees, rainbow-colored flowers in purple, hot pink, light pink, red, orange, yellow, and china blue everywhere, and almost psychedelic rhododendrons. Then the impossibly blue water comes into view with the various types of boats, and my heart wants to jump out of my body!

At the very first stop though, Manh's really close girlfriend, Brandie, gets on the bus with her new boyfriend Chris. They are visiting from Vancouver and came to see the Mariners/Red Sox game. While we were on the bus, we all started having a really fun time joking and laughing. I felt so young again. No one could believe I was almost sixty. I love the shock value of telling them that. They usually think I'm about forty-five. I have to admit I could hear that over and over again, all day long. Brandie told us she had a surgery the day before. She was doing pretty well considering she had a bladder repair. She was about twenty-five, and I could tell she and Manh had a special friendship. I think they went to school together.

We got off the bus in downtown Seattle where there was a lot of excitement due to the Mariners game that night. Manh was determined to find a particular bar to hang out in. I really had to pee and told him it was bad, but he said, "Just a couple more blocks." By then I was sure I was going to wet my pants. I told Brandie I was in trouble, so she grabbed my arm and escorted me up some stairs to a bar where there was a bathroom, and I was saved. I already loved this girl, and when we caught up with Manh and Chris, I scolded them saying, "When a woman says she has to pee, that means *now*, not hold on for one block. You haven't been through childbirth!"

We met up with some friends of Brandie's at the one-block bar. Thank God for cell phones. We all started getting loud and laughing and drinking and eating since it was an Irish pub. In the middle of the conversation I decide to pull off my wig with these people. Mouths dropped to the floor. One of the guys said he couldn't believe what a good wig it was, he couldn't tell at all.

Brandie wanted to put my dark wig on her blonde hair, and it did look pretty cool. Then the waitress came over to our table. She was a beautiful small girl with a buzz cut. Very cool. She told me she had shaved her head for a breast cancer fund-raiser. Girl power! The food was very good, and the beer flowed. Finally we decided to meet up later. Manh wanted to get me to the EMP, which we were supposed to do to begin with. We decided to buy two tickets to the Mariners game that Brandie's boyfriend, Chris, had. Manh called Noble to see if he wanted to go with me to the game, but he said no and that the two of us should use them. *Fine*, who cares about Noble. I was having too much fun with Manh.

There was live music on the street. Right outside the pub was a guy playing the cello. I loved that. We walked to the second level of the building across the street to the monorail that goes right to the EMP. What a spectacular view of downtown Seattle and the water! We arrived at four forty-five, fifteen minutes before it closed for the day. We looked at the gift shop, and I bought a cute T-shirt, and Manh promised to bring me back the next day.

So now we had tickets to the Mariners game. We started walking toward the stadium. How far was it anyway? A long way. My legs were starting to give out. I told Manh, and he said we could get a ride at the edge of the stadium with a rickshaw bike rider who would bring us right up to the stadium. A really vivacious Australian guy saw us waving, and he came lickity split to pick us up. What a relief and how much fun was this! He started pedaling and talking, and they both were treating me like a princess. Life is so good. "Let's get bratwurst and hot dogs. Let's treat the driver!" We flew through the stadium grounds. He knew the best bratwurst. "Oh my god, this is so cool." I'm surrounded by beautiful men just dying to make me so happy—whatever I want. Bratwurst with Dijon mustard and beer tastes so good. Time for the game. The driver of the bike drops us off as close to our seats as you can get.

Now we have to climb up high to our seats, which are perched right above the pitcher's mound. I love our seats. There is an older couple seated next to us, and I tell them about this book. Oh, they want to read it, so I give them my card. I'm selling books all across the country. I bet I'm on Oprah. The game starts off with a bang. The Mariners are holding their own, but things start going downhill. After the seventh inning, Manh starts losing interest. I don't blame him. It's hard to watch your home team lose. I'm losing interest too. Manh says, "Let's go, beat the crowd, and go across the street to a bar and get a drink." It's starting to cool down, so I order a coffee with Bailey's—yummy! A lot of young men are staring at me. I love hanging out with young people; I feel as young as they do. The rest of our group shows up, and after much laughing and hilarity, we all agree to call it a night. Manh and I take Brandie and Chris to their hotel. Brandie and I agree to stay in touch because she wants to write a cookbook and I can help her get published.

When we get to the house, I call Noble because he's supposed to spend the night. He's changed his mind. He needs to keep working on the house. What the fuck? Is he trying to avoid me?

I'm pissed off. Poor Manh has to listen to the ranting of a sexually deprived woman. Manh starts defending him right away. He's an engineer; they all think alike. He's afraid to commit. I don't want commitment; I want to be free and single! I just want sex from him. I wish he weren't so sexy. Manh finally admits Noble's nuts. If he could have our arrangement, he would be thrilled. We finally call it quits. Tomorrow we will try the EMP again.

I wake up at ten thirty and call Noble. He's going to bring Copper River salmon for dinner, so I will see him tonight. He will cook for all of us. That makes me happy. I am so easy to please. Throw me a crumb, that's enough. I wake sleepyhead Manh up, and he wants another half hour. I get ready, and then I wake him up again. He takes a while to get ready, but the wait is worth it because we go to downtown Bellingham, which is the "new downtown" of Seattle. He takes me to the most amazing restaurant for sushi because he knows I love it. I've never had sushi like that; it was just incredible, the best I've ever had. It came around on a conveyer belt that went around the perimeter of the serving area. I was like a kid in a candy store. Anything you want when you see it. Talk about instant gratification. You grab it, and it's yours. Phenomenal!

Manh wants to get me DHEA, the only over-the-counter steroid still available. After he pays the bill for our lunch, he wants to go across the street to a health food store. I wait in the car. He gets me the one formulated for women. What a special guy. He bought that for me because I had told him how serious I was about curing my MS through diet. I was even drinking about an ounce of my own urine every day. Urine is sterile and has a natural steroid in it. He said if I could do that, he knew I was serious. It is disgusting to drink urine. I had to plug my nose and then drink something strong tasting afterward like juice or kombucha, the miracle tea fermented from a mushroom. It has billions of probiotics and all the B vitamins occurring naturally in the fermentation process. I love kombucha; it was one of the secrets to my healing from cancer. We tried for the EMP again, but we ran out of time again. The two of us started walking away and talking. We will wait until I get back from China. There was a people's park that had beautiful flowers and benches to sit and rest. While we were talking, I just started to cry again knowing that things were not going to be what I thought they would be on my trip to China with Noble. Manh was very sympathetic and gave me a hug and emphasized again that engineers are a strange breed. He's an engineer too, but he is an artist as well, so he's well rounded, well adjusted. After a while we started walking toward the monorail and eventually we were back at the house.

Noble did show up with the Copper River salmon, and it was good, but he looked awful with some huge baggie shorts and a tank top. He looked disheveled and tired. Manh fixed asparagus with olive oil and balsamic vinegar to put on the grill with the salmon. I felt disconnected from Noble even more, and I knew he wasn't going to spend the night because we were leaving for Beijing early in the morning. I don't think he was even packed yet. When he left, I did some rearranging in my suitcase, packed up my computer, and went to bed. Our flight was sometime in the early morning.

When I woke up, I wanted to tell Manh something. I walked to his closed bedroom door and stared at it for a long time. Then I knocked and opened it. Manh was partially awake and said, "What's going on?" I crawled in bed with him, and he let me cuddle up to his warm body. We were in the spooning mode when I started to cry again and told him how much he meant to me because of who he was and how he treated me, like a princess. I told him I thought he was pretty close to perfect and that I had fallen in love with him and what an amazing guy I thought he was. I thanked him with all my heart for the wonderful time he had shown me while I was in Seattle. Manh said, "You're welcome, Ginny." Then I got up and got dressed and ready for China.

Beijing, China

The plane we flew on to Beijing was my introduction to the magnificence of China. We flew on Hainan Airlines, which had only been flying out of Seattle for a short time, maybe a month or two. My airline ticket cost $850, which I thought was a real bargain.

We learned this was only the forth flight this plane had ever made. It seemed opulent to me. The plane smelled like a new car. All the seats were upholstered in red embroidered fabric, not silk, but luxurious. The flight attendants wore beautiful royal blue—China Blue uniforms. The girls' uniforms had embroidered flowers on the top and skirt. The male flight attendants were clean cut and well dressed in their China Blue suits. I connected right away with Angela and Eric; I considered them my personal fight attendants because that's how they treated me, as if I was their most important passenger. I was in heaven. We were all given red socks, blankets, pillows, and even toothpaste and toothbrushes. I sat in my assigned seat, and Noble sat behind me rather than beside me or across from me. There were plenty of open seats on the plane. I guess that felt like more rejection to me, but what the hell, I was on my way to China. There was no way anything could bring me down. I was on the adventure of a lifetime.

Noble had told me how wonderful the Chinese people are. He had been to China six times already. He and some of his family had been to the Beijing Olympics just two years earlier. That was the time I was starting to feel really sick. I remember because I pretty much watched every bit of the Olympics on TV. I lay around all day and night because I had no energy. How amazing and remarkable that I was now on a plane to Beijing recovered from stage IV breast cancer after sixteen weeks of chemotherapy—a medical miracle. My life is a beautiful, spectacular adventure! I am so grateful for my healing. Angela and Eric were so intrigued with me. I walked back to the kitchen on the plane to talk to them. Just like Noble had told me, the Chinese people love all things American. I told them that I was a flight attendant for Northwest Orient Airlines back in the early 1970s. They didn't understand. How old was I? I asked them to guess how old I was. Eric piped up and said thirty-four. Oh god, I love and adore these people! When I told them I was going to be sixty on my next birthday, they were dumbfounded. The whole time I was in China, the people I came to know considered me a fashion model type. I am 5'10", have very long legs, and am pretty thin, and I really was a fashion model in high school. Voila! I love being known as the fashion model.

I watched four movies, ate two delicious Chinese meals, and drank many glasses of mango juice, coconut juice, and wine with dinner—all compliments of Hainan Airlines. It makes our struggling airlines in the USA seem kind of pathetic. I hope that changes in the future, but it seems unlikely. The twelve-hour flight from Seattle to Beijing ended before I knew it. I had hardly spoken to Noble. Life just kept moving forward, and I was enjoying the ride more than I could ever have imagined. Jenhua was waiting for us at the area designated after we had been through customs. I fell in love with him the moment I met this humble man and heard his determination to speak English. Jenhua and his wife, Sunyen, owned the condominium Noble and I would be living in for the next five weeks, by ourselves.

We arrived at the New House as it came to be known in the weeks to come as opposed to their house downtown where they lived with their fourteen-year-old son nicknamed Dino. The New House was located on the outskirts of Beijing with a view of the mountains. We went on the elevator up to the seventh floor, and the door to the condominium was just to the left as we exited. Two units were on each floor of the ten-story building. Jenhua opened the door for us, and I was blown away by how luxurious, but simple, our living arrangement would be. Everything was white—the floors, the walls, and the furniture. Jenhua gave us a walking tour or maybe it was Noble because he had stayed there a few times before. There was a large living room, a large dining room, a master bedroom with a king-sized bed, two full baths right next to each other, a small second bedroom with a bunk bed, and a small kitchen with stainless steel modular fixtures. There was a washing machine for clothes in a tiny room next to the kitchen. There was no dryer. We would hang our clothes on the lanai that was at the far end of the living room with the gorgeous view of the mountains and other condos that were built all around us.

I settled in by unpacking my suitcase and setting up my bathroom with my toiletries and facial products. The accommodations couldn't have been more beautiful. While I was doing all that, Noble and Jenhua were messing around with the computer, trying to get the Internet and Skype working correctly. That's men for you, electronics first. Jenhua left then to give us some privacy. I wondered what the sleeping arrangement would be. Was Noble going to sleep in the king with me? I don't remember if he slept there the first night, but I know he moved to the top bunk in the small bedroom the next day, confirming that we were not going to be intimate in China. That didn't stop me from trying over and over again. I tolerated rejection again and again because I really couldn't believe now that we were alone again, he wouldn't want me like he had in Colorado Springs. It took me way too long to accept that he had let his psychiatrist influence his feelings about me in a very negative way. Noble was definitely not in touch with his feelings. He was afraid of them. I was used to persevering in my life with men. Why? No one wants rejection. I have always known I'm loveable, but that doesn't take into consideration the complexities of the men I have been with. Noble turned out to be the most complex man I have ever been with.

We rested the next day, and I learned we had an amazing event to look forward to every day—the bird symphony. About 8:00 a.m. every morning I would hear birds singing. I talk about it in the first travelogue e-mail I sent to all my people back home. The third day we were in China we went to see Dr. Li, Jason's personal acupuncturist, at 11:00 a.m. That was one of the most important days of my life. That meeting changed my life forever.

Dr. Li

Dr. Li's office was on the fourth floor in the Zhongjingxin Hotel in downtown Beijing. The hotel was a Communist-run beautiful modern building with a restaurant and incredible gift shop where I bought a lot of beautiful jewelry for very little money. The Chinese clerks came to know me and gave me some very good deals because they saw me every other day for a month or more. They loved me, and I loved them right back. The doormen always had a big smile for me and treated us like royalty when we left each time in a taxi. Noble was always with me when I saw Dr. Li. He witnessed what happened in that office. He witnessed the miracle. I loved the lobby of that hotel. It had marble floors and massive upholstered leather sofas with ornately carved wood bases. We would take the elevator up to his office in the hotel's beauty salon. He would be waiting for us with a big smile on his face always. Dr. Li was a small man; his body was perfectly proportioned. He seemed very young, but I soon realized he had a ten-year-old daughter and a sixteen-year-old son. I figure he was in his late thirties or early forties.

I would always use the modern bathroom when we arrived. That was a treat after all the "squatters" I was using in restaurants and tourist attractions. The room he did my treatment in was beautiful. It had two massage table beds with silk covers trimmed in fringe. There were large windows with lavender silk curtains, which he pulled sheers across when I was lying on the bed. I never wore my shoes or wig during my treatments. I wore long yoga pants so he could feel my body with his velvet hands. That's what I called them because his hands were powerful yet unbelievably gentle while he was exploring my body for places of pain. He definitely found that place of pain, my right hip and across my lower back. He dug so deep; I thought I would pass out from the pain. I taught him a bit of English at that point. I taught him the difference between "a little" and "a lot." That hip area was "a lot" with every dig he made.

After a half hour of reflexology on my feet and a half hour of deep tissue massage on my body, he proceeded to put many needles in my hip, hands, feet, and ankles. That process took another half hour. I loved all of it except the painful hip part, which was excruciating. Dr. Li was very attentive to my happiness level. He would ask me several times during and after my treatment if I was happy. I would always answer, "I'm *so* happy." He loved to hear me say that, and he would repeat "*so* happy" with a big smile on his face. I think he acted a lot like the Dalai Lama, just silly, and always animated and interested in how I felt. The other word he knew and understood was *beautiful.* That was the word he used to describe me every single visit, and he used it many times. He made me feel as if I was his most special patient. Dr. Li infused me with love, happiness, and light every time I visited his office. What a lucky girl! We were a team, Dr. Li and I. He is one of my most meaningful symbols because of what he did for me.

Dr. Li the third day I was in China

After that first visit, I felt so invigorated; I told Noble and Jenhua, who were waiting on a sofa outside the door, that I felt like going to the Forbidden City. Dr. Li said I could do whatever I felt like, so after many thanks, we headed out of his office to have an adventure and lesson in ancient Chinese history. Jenhua drove us to the Forbidden City and dropped Noble and me off to be on our own.

Lily approached us as Jenhua was pulling away. She wanted to know if we wanted to hire her as an interpreter and a guide inside the city. I was immediately drawn to her. She was adorable in her frayed beige baseball hat embroidered with *Berkeley* and *Los Angeles*, cute pants, and denim jacket with white T-shirt underneath. Her English was very good, pretty close to perfect. Noble wasn't sure about hiring her, but I was. He asked if she was a student, and she shot back, "What you think, that I don't know more than a student?" She handed him her professional tour guide card. This young girl spoke to my heart. I wanted to help her. I liked her immediately, and it just got better from there. She amazed me. "Where did you learn English?" I asked. "Oh, by myself." Really? No college or formal study. That was impressive. Noble put a deposit down on a wheelchair for me. Off we went to see the Forbidden City. There is no other word than *magnificent* to describe it. I was captivated by her knowledge of all the ancient dynasties and history of China. We were under her care for about two hours, including tea together at the teahouse while we waited for the rain to let up. I bought a very beautiful rice paper wall hanging with some red Chinese calligraphy on it. I asked Lily what it meant, and she told me the symbols stood for longevity and happiness. I loved that, and she helped me bargain the price down a little bit. We parted company because we were all tired. I promised to call her on her cell phone and plan another day of sightseeing. Noble called Jenhua, and he picked us up and dropped us at the New House.

Lily and me at The Forbidden City

I lay down on the white sofa, shut my eyes, and listened to my iTunes, totally relaxed after a very remarkable day. I was thinking what a fortunate, lucky girl I was to be experiencing China with Noble. The phone rang at the house, and Noble answered it. He listened to what Jason was saying and then walked over to the sofa. He looked me in the eyes and told me something that absolutely blew my mind. Noble said, "Jason says, Dr. Li says Ginny has a pinched nerve deep in her groin. He says she's had it for a very long time. Noble, she doesn't have multiple sclerosis. It was never MS. It's a pinched nerve. It's always been a pinched nerve. He says he needs to see her twelve times to fix the problem." I just stared at Noble. I don't know what I was feeling. It was surreal for sure. Noble handed me the phone so I could talk to Jason. He explained everything all over again. I asked him about our trip to Kashgar. I told him I really wanted to go there. We already had the whole trip planned and paid for. This was my special trip that Noble agreed to. He wasn't interested in traveling outside of Beijing since he had already been there five or six times and traveled everywhere he wanted to go. He told me I could pick one place I wanted to go. Can you imagine being in a strange country with none of your immediate family and being told you don't have a very serious disease that you thought you had for twenty-two years? Oh my god, talk about rocking my world. Now I was on a natural high, which I was pretty sure would never go away. I went from a life of compromised health and pain to a close-to-perfect disease-free new life after one phone call.

The reason I picked Kashgar was because my special friend, Meggie, told me about it. She happened to be at a party in Scottsdale, Arizona, where she lives, and she met a writer for the *New York Times* magazine. He wrote for the travel section. She must have told him she had friends going to China, and he told her about Kashgar. He told her to tell us that if there was any way we could get there to go because it won't be the same in a couple of years. He told her it was like leaving one world and entering another. That's all she had to tell me, and I knew I wanted to go there. I told Noble that was where I wanted to go for my one place. He researched it. I did the same, and he agreed that we could go there. Traveling to Kashgar was a big undertaking because it was as far away from Beijing as you could get, way on the other side of China on the Pakistan/Kazakhstan border. It was a four-and-a-half-hour flight from Beijing, like flying from New York to Los Angeles. For the return from Kashgar, Noble thought it might be fun to take the train from Kashgar to Urumugi involving an overnight, a twenty-four-hour trip through the mountains and desert of China. We would then spend a night and day in the city and then fly back to Beijing on a two-hour flight.

Jason arranged my next twelve visits with Dr. Li. I would see him three times before we went to Kashgar and then nine times when I returned. My appointments were always the same, every other day at 11:00 a.m. Noble went with me every time and paid my bill with money he collected from me ahead of time because he wanted to make sure there was money to pay Dr. Li. He charged the equivalent of $48 for each visit.

Kashgar

We exited the airport in Kashgar with our luggage in hand and started looking for our prearranged driver and guide that Jenhua had helped find for us at a very low cost. He knew people in the travel business. After about half an hour we spotted the driver. There weren't many people at the airport, so we kind of figured out which car it was, and they knew us because we were the only Americans: a 5'10" gal and a blond guy. The two of us were really quite an oddity. There weren't many of us around this part of the world, like zero. I never saw another American in Kashgar—some French men and one Brit woman, but that was all I ever saw from the Western world. It was remarkable to be the only Americans! It made one feel special because they love America there.

The car was a new burgundy Volkswagen sedan with our driver who spoke only a little English and our guide, Musajian, who spoke English very well. He was a handsome nineteen-year-old Muslim boy who looked like he could be my son. His uncle Abdul owned the travel agency in Seiman Hotel, where we were staying. Musajian was slender and dark haired with big brown eyes and

135

very beautiful sculptured features. He looked Irish with a slight Mongolian slant to his eyes. After we got to know each other, I did feel like he was my son, the one I never had. He became my friend and confidant as I became to him as I learned his remarkable story. Musa was a very special and intelligent boy. He was an only child and was mostly raised by his six uncles. The family was of the ethnic group the Uyghers, Muslims who live in harmony with all other people living in Kashgar. On the streets of Kashgar everyone looks different—Muslims, Chinese, Turks, Russians, Mongolians, Pakistanis, and Kazakhstanis. I saw Muslim women in full garb with only their eyes showing and the contrast of young Chinese girls wearing the most current fashion clothing and shoes. I bought some of the most beautiful clothing for my grandchildren at the shop in Seiman Hotel. For myself I bought a gorgeous high-fashion red silk jacket and a necklace made out of hand-carved coral beads from the river and hand-carved camel-bone beads from the desert. I had fun bargaining the price down to a place where I felt I was getting a good deal, and the very classy shopkeeper was happy too.

While we were driving to Seiman Hotel, Musajian asked us how our trip was. He asked how old I thought he was. I said twenty, and he said no, nineteen. So I asked him how old he thought I was. The youngest yet, thirty-two! He thought Noble was about forty-two. I love this game of guessing. I keep getting younger, that's the best! We pulled up into the hotel, which was magical with a beautiful lobby with well-worn furniture and some beautiful art pieces of jade. Everything seemed to be hand-carved on the walls and woodwork. We met Musa's uncle Abdul and were given a tour of the place by Musa. I noticed all the beautiful flowers everywhere—roses in all colors of pink and red. Our room was truly amazing. The more I looked at the walls and the ceiling, the more I was amazed at the craftsmanship and intricacies of the painting and carving and attention to details. We rested for a few hours and then Musajian came to get us for dinner. We walked across the street from the hotel to a wonderful restaurant with a patio. We had our own little room off the main dining room that was very intimate. We feasted on lamb kebabs, egg, and tomato dish, which was outstanding; we as also had a vegetable dish that was as fresh and fragrant as you could possibly imagine. Musajian did the tea in his special way where he rinsed the first small amount around his cup, poured it into his own, and then poured again into ours. After dinner we went back to Seiman and made plans to go to the grand market at ten in the morning.

That night I experienced some of the worst pain I've ever had. I don't know why so much pain now. Maybe it was because the nerves were waking up from the residual pain of detoxing from the chemo drug taxetere, which I had sixteen rounds of starting way back in December. My oncologist did not prepare me for how severe the pain would be, but it was bad, bad, bad. I don't know if I went to sleep, but at some point I was keenly aware that things were getting worse. I had intense burning in both legs and lots of cramping spasms. I couldn't help it; I just started crying. I woke Noble and told him I needed help with getting warm damp towels for my legs. That's what Dr. Li said to do for pain. Maybe I slept for a little while, but then I woke up with close-to-unbearable pain. Noble just *freaked out*! "I'm calling Jason!" No answer. "I'm calling Jenhua to call Jason. We should go back to Beijing. This is serious. Jenhua thinks we should go the hospital." "The hospital? I don't need the hospital. I need a Xanax." I didn't bring them. I've been doing so well. "Come on, we're going to the hospital." Nobel goes to the lobby to find a cab. This is crazy. I don't even put my wig on—we are going to the hospital. It's 1:30 a.m. We drive through a deserted town. I am numb. Noble says he should have never brought me here. He only did it because I wanted it so much.

We pull into the hospital entrance, and it looks like a war zone, not a hospital. I don't like this at all. We are not even sure it's a hospital. The road is all torn up with big chunks of concrete all around. We drive on a very bumpy surface and then we come to an entrance. It's almost totally dark inside with no sign of life except one guy behind glass, speaking to someone on the other side. What the hell am I doing here? This is ridiculous. I feel like I'm in a hospital in Nazi Germany. Noble is on the phone with Jenhua. Has he spoken to Jason? No. Noble is standing in line waiting for the guy behind the glass. *No more obedient girl!* I walk up to Noble and tell him I don't want to be there. I don't like it here.

I'm not staying here. Jenhua wants to talk to me. "Why don't you stay, Ginny?" "Jenhua, this is not a life or death situation. This is pain. That is all. I will handle it." Noble gets help finding a cab back to the hotel. Off we go back to the hotel. My legs feel a little better now that the circulation is flowing.

After flagging a guy down inside the grounds of the hotel to unlock the gate, we go up to the room. Noble starts losing it *big-time.* "We are going back to Beijing, first flight out in the morning." He tells me he can't deal with my pain. He feels helpless and says he can't help me. I stare at the ceiling and then I have a moment of clarity. I ask Noble if I am paying the extra expense of the flight back. He says yes, and asks me if I don't think that's only fair. *No.* I'm not making any of the decisions here, and I don't want to miss any of this trip. He says we will lose all the money on everything that has been prepaid. He yells at me, "There is not going to be any discussion. We are going back. That's it."

Silence. "Listen, Noble, I want to say something and don't interrupt me. You aren't letting me have any part of this conversation, if that's what you call it. I am not being true to myself with you. I am walking on eggshells around you. I'm afraid to say this or that because Noble won't love me if he doesn't agree. If I act a way that bugs him, he won't love me. Well, I don't care anymore. I'm not letting you control me, Noble. I'm a great person, and I love myself. Yes, I love everything about you. I love the way you smile, the way you smell, the way you look, and that you are courteous, caring, and ethical. I love you. That's my gift to you. I'm not changing one thing about this trip. If you want to go back to Beijing, I'll stay here by myself. I'll be fine. And you are wrong. There is something you can do for me. You could stay in the same bed with me, you could put your arms around me, and we could make love. All those things would really help my pain." "I can't do any of that." "Yes, you can. You just won't. That's it." "Okay, I will stay. I would never leave you here alone."

"Okay then, let's go to bed, and I'll get a foot massage in the morning, and we'll go to the market at ten with Musajian." "Okay," he says. I'm feeling a little better, so I think one more round of hot towels might help with circulation, and he helps me with that.

The rooster crows about 5:00 a.m. Noble comments from the other double bed. We start out as friends as though nothing happened. The Chinese/Mongolian girl comes at eight to give me my foot massage. She is quite beautiful and voluptuous with a low cut tank top and stylish jacket and cargo pants with embroidery. She brings her own wooden bucket to soak my feet in. She fills it with hot water from the bathtub and then sprinkles flower petals in it. I lie on the bed and let her work her magic on my feet and legs. She has powerful hands and is a trained reflexologist. I'm in heaven for a full hour, and then we try to communicate without a common language. I smile at her and pay her the equivalent of $9 in yuan and say one of my few Chinese words, Xie Xie, meaning "thank you."

Musajian and the driver are there at 10:00 a.m. "Let's go. The market is not far away." We are dropped off where the food starts. There is the smell of shish kebabs everywhere grilling on outside fires. We buy a few lamb kebabs and dumplings for one yuan. They are crazy delicious. There are fountains of pomegranate juice, apricot juice, and coconut juice. We buy a large glass of the pomegranate juice for the equivalent of eighty cents. Kashgar is the pomegranate capital of the world. We wander into the covered tent market and find a stall with forty different varieties of almonds plus dried apricots, figs, melons, and grapes. Incredible! We buy some almonds to take with us as a snack, and I find some sheepskin hats for my grandkids. I start to get the shopping fever. We leave the covered area and walk around a very large mosque. On a special prayer day, fifty thousand men can pray in the area in front and spilling off to the side streets. Mosques are where all Muslim men pray, so serenity, seriousness, and cleanliness are requested. There are a number of taboos in the Islam religion. There must be no hurting of flowers or plants when passing by. Looking on and laughing at the prayers is not permitted. There is no excreting around the kitchen or the room for fetching and storing water. Uyghers are prohibited from taking pork, blood, dead animals, fierce animals, fierce birds, donkey, mule, and camel.

Much of what I was feeling during this time is recorded in my journal and a stream of e-mails I was sending to all my friends and family as a travelogue of the trip. However, I want to explain more of what happened in Kashgar with Musajian and me. The two of us spent some very special time together. He became like a son to me, the one I never had. We just connected from the very first day we met. We spent an entire day and evening together without Noble. I wanted to be apart from Noble because our lack of intimacy was starting to wear on me. He made it easy because he had his own plans in Kashgar. That was his business.

Kashgar

May 28

Well, I don't know if everyone is ready for this story, but here goes. We are visiting the most interesting and beautiful city you can possibly imagine. Yesterday was a day of smells of food, the most delicious food I have ever had. This food encompasses the real meaning of slow food. It is organically grown, no pesticides in the most pristine mountain air, and cooked from scratch as you order. We went to the peoples market outdoors. These people are totally self sufficient. They make everything. Imagine fountains of fresh mango juice, pomegranate,and oconut. This is the pomegranate capital of the world. The smell of fresh lamb sish kebobs would knock you out. Oceans of fresh almonds and nuts, roasted or not is just intoxicating. I am an oddity here, that's for sure. Everyone shyly stares at me so I always flash a big smile and then they smile big back at me. The men look and then talk to each other. I can only guess what they are saying. They stare at Noble too. We are the only foreigners that I have seen in the market. I'm so tall and they are fascinated by the way I look. I am fascinated by the way they look . Everyone looks completely different. Some women have traditional Muslim garb, younger ones are fashionable. There are as many Chinese and Mongolians some in their tradtional garb, younger ones not. Lots of babies have shaved heads and look like baby Buddhas. They really cherish them because they only have one, so they are all dressed with beautiful shoes and designer clothing. After the food we go to the artisans market where everything is handmade, often right there in front of you. I started buying some really incredible things for very little money. They love to barter and so do I. I'm having a blast while Noble and our guide, Musajon look on and throw their two cents in. We walk on and Musajon spots a guy out in the open and says he does the traditional medicine of the yugirs. We step closer and I see that his whole hand is covered with scorpions and there is a big live toad in front of him and snakes writhing around and he is selling an elixir for pain made out of all these things. He beckons me to sit down and he wants me to pull up my pant leg so he can brush on part of the bottle. I figure what the heck, I had horrible leg pain last night, why not give it a try. He said it would work in a few minutes but I didn't notice any difference so we left and I didn't buy any. As I walked, I noticed that my one leg was feeling less and less pain. Musajohn ran back and bought a bottle for about fifty cents. We listened to music kind of like Ravi Shankar with their traditional handmade instruments. I was mesmerized. I used the scorpion medicine last night and finally got a good nights sleep. Pictures to follow. Love, the miracle girl.

Ginny Wesley

140

Musajian picked me up with the electric scooter, and we went exploring in the old city of Kashgar. The Chinese government is taking this ancient city down brick by brick, which are in piles everywhere one looks in Kashgar. They don't value anything that isn't strictly Chinese, like the Uygher's and their culture, which of course, is Muslim. Musa explained how the people still live in this old city, and we actually went deep into their neighborhoods and experienced the smells of grilled lamb and other dishes of vegetables and fruits being served from vendors on the street. We passed many little children who wanted to use the only word in English they knew—"Hello, hello" to answer my greeting of "Nihau." Musa told me of his dreams to become a doctor in his village after the destruction of Kashgar by the Chinese is finished. I think he dreamed of coming to America to have a better life too. Then he told me how he was the only nineteen-year-old boy in his village because the Chinese came in and did an ethnic cleansing of all the baby boys the year he was born. His six uncles took him and raised him. He told me how he loved his mother very much, and he is her only child, but she would love for him to go to America for a better life even if it meant leaving her. Musa and I e-mail each other almost every day. I'm trying to get him here. I believe he will come to America eventually and become a doctor. He is a brilliant boy.

After the old city we went to an amusement park high on a hill above the People's Park where there was a statue of Mao, the past leader admired by most Chinese people. It was a little difficult getting up there, but we made it with me walking part of the way and Musa finessing the scooter up the steep hill. Once we got up there we had a spectacular view of Kashgar, and we rode the giant Ferris wheel that we could see from miles away. When we got back to the Seiman, Musa dropped me off to have a little rest. He came back to the room later so the three of us could go out to dinner at the most beautiful restaurant I have ever been in right across the street from the hotel.

The restaurant was built, as Musa explained, by one wealthy Uygher man who apparently inherited money somehow. I have never seen so much opulence in one place. The floors were marble and all the furniture was hand carved. There was balcony seating as well as on the main floor. We were seated up in the balcony. The marble staircase with hand-carved railings on both sides was the centerpiece of the restaurant. There were two giant cylinder-shaped fish tanks on either side with huge orange coy swimming inside. An enormous ornate chandelier hung from the center ceiling over the staircase. Musa did the ordering of the food. He was the expert and connoisseur of all things delectable. First we had tea in his special fashion and then the dishes started arriving one by one. First came roasted peanuts, and then an egg and tomato dish that we ordered many times in the days to come because both Noble and I loved it. We had delicious fried fish and vegetables sliced impossibly thin and so fresh and crispy that my mouth just watered with every bite. It was about this time that I became aware of the fact that my taste buds had come back in triplicate since the chemotherapy had ended in April. I was so grateful to be having this heightened experience in China, where the food is so remarkably good, so fresh, so healthy. I was on an

143

anti-inflammatory diet with no effort at all. We finished up the meal with delicious homemade ice cream made right there at the restaurant every day.

Musa came up to the room to view all the purchases I had made in Kashgar. I had laid them all out on the bed before we went to dinner. He admired everything from the beautiful red silk jacket to the hand-carved and engraved chef's knife I bought for Chas at the artisan's market. We all made plans to be together in the morning the next day because our train was leaving in the late afternoon for Urumuqi. I was having one final reflexology appointment with Condoliz at 8:00 a.m. and Noble would be gone doing whatever he did without me.

The rooster crowed at 5:00 a.m. as usual, and Noble and I slept another couple of hours and then began our last day in my favorite city. Condoliz came as Noble left for breakfast downstairs, compliments of Abdul and Seiman Hotel. She admired all my treasures from Kashkar and then gave me an amazing foot massage. She finished with complete coverage of my legs and feet with the Scorpion water to take away the neuropathic pain from the chemo drugs that were still circulating in my body. Noble showed up about ten with a couple of fourteen-year-old Chinese girls that he met at People's Park where the Mao statue stood. Their father gave them permission to have ice cream with us at the beautiful restaurant. They were completely enamored with me and wanted pictures of the four of us for their family. They were adorable and wanted to practice their English. The three of us shoved together in the booth. Noble and Musa sat across from us. We all ate ice cream, and Noble treated all of us when the bill came.

Musa and I left on the electric scooter to get a new battery for my camera, and then our driver drove us to the train station. I tried to bring Chas's knife in my bag, but they took it out, so I had to leave it with Musa. I still don't have it because he can't send it in the mail either. I did get the Scorpion medicine through, which was very useful for the rest of my stay in Beijing. I hated saying good-bye to Musa, and he later sent me the following e-mail:

Hi

Sat, May 30, 2009 at 1:21 AM

I had a wonderful time with you...I can't stop myself frist I leave you at station...I love you guy's you're very good to me
my heart is crying now..when I call you on the way I can't stop my tears....come on take care of urself

---

Sun, May 31, 2009 at 3:53 AM

We are in Urumqi now and are staying at a very beautiful 5 star hotel. The train ride was awesome and comfortable. We will go out to eat at a Muslim restaurant in the hotel. Then I want to go to the nightclub in the hotel. I will take a bath tonight with flower petals. I will never forget how much fun it was to be with you, Masajian. You are a very special person, never change, okay? I'm already dreaming of next year with my family and friends. We will e-mail many times over the next year. Love and Kisses, Ginny

---

I started writing in my journal knowing that I was going to explode at Noble as soon as we were moving along on the train. I felt like a volcano ready to erupt at any moment. I had been pushing down my feelings for way too long. I had thought about going home early. I had tried so hard with Noble. He was playing games, and I didn't know which ones. It wasn't worth it to feel rejected all the time for no reason. I knew I had the ability to fire him up and fast, but he just couldn't accept love from me. Why? Was it because of his mother? It seemed like his attachment to her was unhealthy. What did I know? The thrill was definitely gone. I didn't want to be there for another three and a half weeks like that. There were a few more things I wanted to do in Beijing and then I would be ready to go home. I decided I would talk to Jason and Dr. Li about leaving my treatment early. I was unhappy and wanted to be with my family. I was used to having more love in my life. It felt kind of sterile emotionally.

Noble climbed up on the top bed in our cabin, and no one else came in, so we had the whole space to ourselves. I tried to sleep as it got darker outside, but I had a hard time during the night with the pain in my legs. I tried everything in my bag of tricks—the Scorpion

145

water, the Chinese herbs I had specially ordered from Mountain Mama's in the Springs, and finally just resorted to shedding a few tears. I didn't wake Noble because his position was the same: he couldn't help me, as he hammered home to me many times—no hugs, no kisses, no intimacy.

It finally started to get bright outside, and I was excited to see the mountains. Noble climbed down and sat across from me. He was pleasant as always, and we started enjoying the scenery outside the train window together. At first it was desert mountains like Phoenix, only bigger. Next we saw a big river and dromedary camels with the two humps, and everything started looking like an oasis. We saw bigger and bigger mountains, some with a little snow on top, and giant boulders in the river like Glenwood Springs and the Colorado. Another train passed. We went through some very long tunnels, way longer than Vail. I couldn't help but think of the manpower it took to build those tunnels. One thing China does not lack is manpower. We saw herds of sheep and horses with tails to the ground.

I decide to go to the diner car for breakfast, and Noble comes along. Noble won't eat. He is getting weirder and weirder. He won't accept tea even when the adorable girl brings it for free. We start talking about friends, and I ask him, "How are we going to resolve this situation?" I decide I will definitely talk to Jenhua and Jason when we get back to Beijing. The train is pulling into the station in Urumuqi, and we hustle to get our bags ready to disembark. Noble has a map of the city, and we try to show the cab driver where our five-star hotel is. It is called The Mirage, and when we get there, I can't believe how opulent it is. It reminds me of The Broadmoor Hotel at home. Behind the front desk was a long wall of carved white jade. There was another wall, two stories high and forty feet wide, with carvings in jade of all the great manmade wonders of the world. It was weeping water that went down into a pool two stories down. The whole building was constructed of marble floors, pillars, and walls. Just remarkable. Our room was ultra luxurious with free Internet, TV with a selection of forty-five movies, and Jacuzzi bathtub.

I took a nap while Noble explored, and when he came back, we decided to have dinner at the Muslim restaurant, one of four or five in the hotel. He wanted me to choose, and I made a mistake by ordering fish. It didn't taste good, but we had dumplings and vegetables that were delicious; then we both decided to get out of there and go back to the room. I was restless during the night, and my legs hurt. Then I started having intestinal cramps and dry mouth. Just like a morning in Kashgar, I was having another total colonic evacuation. Noble said he had some problems after dinner. Shit! We got food poisoning from that fish. I had to power through the cramps and nausea and wait it out until my body was done. Noble went to breakfast and brought some yogurt back to the room. I just shoveled the yogurt in because we wanted to go to the museum where the mummies were. We were told they had mummies two thousand years old that were perfectly preserved and standing upright because they were caught in a sandstorm and completely covered from head to toe when they were discovered. Unfortunately we never saw them because the museum was closed on Mondays. We ended up shopping until our plane left in the late afternoon. I loved that because there were some beautiful designer shops nearby that I could bargain in. I bought Noble a pair of pants that he really liked when he returned from an errand so we could have ice cream at the new Radisson Hotel in the same shopping mall.

At the airport I was filmed by a couple of young Chinese girls working for the airline. Noble thought they might use it to advertise their handicap accessibility—Pretty girl in a wheelchair with a big smile on her face, waving at the camera. Jenhua was there to pick us up after our two-and-a-half-hour flight into Beijing. I was happy to be back to the New House after the weeklong adventure in Kashgar. I had an appointment with Dr. Li at my usual eleven time slot the following morning.

Noble and I walked to the bus stop one block from the condo. We boarded the 333 bus, which took us past the Summer Palace to the next stop, where we waited for the next bus that took us closer to Dr. Li's office in the Communist hotel. Once we got to that stop we took a cab the rest of the way for about $5 or about thirty yuan. The doorman was all smiles for us, and we headed through the lobby and up to the fifth floor where Dr. Li was waiting for us. He was very interested in our trip, so I tried to communicate with him through my enthusiasm. I showed him the Scorpion water, and he did not like the smell at all. I don't think he knew anything about Kashgar. I learned from Jenhua that they were all worried about us going to Kashgar. I don't think they understood why we wanted to go there. They all had a fear of the Muslims, including Jason. Funny how I ended up loving Musa so much. Musa did worship at the mosque with the other Muslim men. I asked him if he believed in the Muslim idea of the forty virgins if you died a martyr, and he said yes. Noble told me later that he thought Musa would turn against his religion when he learned more about the world situation.

I was so happy to be back in Dr. Li's powerful hands. It was just heaven having him massaging my feet and body. He was magic to me. He infused me with healing, happiness, love, and a special form of intimacy I really needed. He also told me I was *so* beautiful many times during my treatments. What girl doesn't want to hear that on a regular basis? Noble was waiting in the hallway outside the room, and when my treatment was finished, he came in and told me Jason had called. He would pick us up outside the hotel, and we would go for lunch at his house with Sandra and baby Justin. I was so happy to finally meet Jason. I had spoken to him on the phone quite a few times, and we connected right away. I could tell he had a big personality like mine, so meeting him was fantastic.

He pulled up in his giant-sized black Audi with blackout windows right in front of the hotel complex. It almost felt like we were very important people. We were actually, to Jason. Noble was his best friend, and I was in because Noble had chosen me to bring to China. That's how I got in to see Dr. Li. He was Jason's own personal acupuncturist. Jason had a beautiful deep voice, and his English was impeccable. The whole family was in the car, including Sandra and Justin in the top of the line American baby car seat. I sat in front with Jason, and Noble sat in the back with Sandra and his godson, Justin. The plan was to have lunch and then relax all afternoon with them and then go to dinner at the finest Taiwanese restaurant in Beijing. Sandra was Taiwanese, and she was connected to the owner in some way. I loved Sandra right away. She was beautiful and quirky and reminded me of a modern day Lucille Ball.

Their condo was located in a complex where many officials from the Communist Party lived. We were instructed to dash into the building as soon as Jason dropped us all in front of the door, so no one would see us. We weren't supposed to be there as American tourists. Jason and Sandra were building a big house on the outskirts of Beijing in a wealthy community with all the amenities. The condo was similar to ours, only bigger. One whole room was set up like a huge playpen for Justin. His toys were in large see-through plastic storage bins all around the perimeter of the room. There was a large flat-screen TV from where he could watch children's videos. He was allowed to watch only American English language material like Baby Einstein and Sesame Street. The only Chinese he ever heard in the house was from the nanny and the female cook. Jason and Sandra spoke only English to Justin.

We had a wonderful lunch of traditional Chinese dishes with a variety of vegetables and rice and meat. Sandra wanted to eat alone so she could concentrate on her food while we played with Justin. I let Noble get in the playpen with Justin alone while I sat outside and watched godfather and godson connect. It was nice, and I was able to pay attention to some of the lovely details in their home. I loved the oversized professional photograph of Jason and a pregnant Sandra laughing together resting on an easel in a corner of the room. When Sandra finished her lunch, we retired into Jason's office. He finished up all his business so he could give us his complete attention. Jason is a magnificent person. He is small in stature like most Chinese men, but he seemed bigger than life because he just emanated an excitement about life. He matched me with his enthusiasm and love of life.

We were like soul mates. He just got me and told me I was so beautiful too, just like Dr. Li. I have to say I loved those moments of male attention. We started talking about sex and monogamy. At first I strongly expressed my belief in monogamy, but then I realized I didn't feel that strongly about it anymore. I just knew I wanted a lot more of it since I got my life back. Making up for lost time I guess. Jason was a financial investment banker now, and I got the impression that he wanted to make as much money as he possibly could and then leave China and bring his family to America for good.

The conversation was so stimulating for me that time just evaporated. It was time to pack baby up and the nanny and go downtown for our dinner reservation. We all snuck out to the car that Jason pulled around again with me in front. The nanny sat on the floor in the back. The Taiwanese restaurant was located in a very upscale mall with beautiful shops on all sides, below and above. The dinner was just incredible. If I remember correctly, we had twelve different kinds of dumplings all piled on top of one another in the straw steam baskets. We were served several different varieties of meat along with the usual mouthwatering beautifully presented vegetables. The nanny put the bones on the marble floor of this beautiful restaurant. Sandra rolled her eyes at Jason and looked so disgusted. Jason explained that she didn't know any better because she came from farmers. Sandra scolded her and told her to pick them up and take baby Justin for a walk outside the restaurant in the mall. Dessert was the crowning glory for this meal. Sandra had specially ordered her favorite delight from Taiwan. A large bowl was placed on the table with a mound that was covered in fresh sliced mangoes. Sandra served us in individual bowls. As she spooned onto the mound, the center was revealed—it was shaved ice so white and fluffy that it seemed to be ice cream. OMG, I just couldn't get enough! We were all reaching the point of exhaustion, so Noble and I took the subway home so Jason wouldn't have to drive another forty-five minutes to get us home. The subway was in the lower level of the mall. Piece of cake.

At a taiwanese restaurant with Sandra, Jason and their son Justin

We rested with the exception of lunch with Jenhua. Another culinary delight. We all shared a huge bowl of chicken with rice noodles. It had tiny eggs floating in it, which were cooked in the hot stock. After we finished, we went across the street to the most amazing bakery called *cake*. I started making a habit of going there when we ate close by because they had incredible treats for very little money, and Noble and I could share them for the next few days. I was in the process of getting more money wired into my account, and it was slightly stressful because Noble seemed worried about me paying Dr. Li. I knew it wasn't a problem because my bank had approved it, but there was a waiting period.

Noble and I started to have acupuncture with Dr. Li together. He lost about 30 percent of his vision in one eye during the Olympics. A blood vessel burst in his eye. I fell fast asleep while Noble was having his treatment and I had needles in my hip, hands, and feet. When I woke up Dr. Li was calling his sixteen-year-old son at boarding school. He put the phone to my ear so his son could speak English to me. He said he was pleased to meet me, and we chatted for a little while. This pleased Dr. Li greatly. Noble and I went to lunch, and then I took a cab all the way home. My legs hurt and ached, and my ankles were swollen. I was detoxing big-time from the chemo. While I was resting on the sofa, Noble called and said Jason, Sandra, Jenhua, and Sunyen were coming over for a cocktail party the next day at three thirty. Noble and I whipped the New House into shape for the next day, and when they arrived, we were ready. I had turned the master bedroom into a showcase of all my treasures from Kashgar. Jason told me that he finally understood why I loved Kashgar so much. It was the mixing of cultures with much influence from the Western world when Genghis Khan and the like formed the Silk Road. Kashgar was a giant oasis, desert, glacier, and had snow-crowned mountains. It was a key spot on the old Silk Road to link the Western world with the East.

Jenhua and Sunyen arrived first, so I had some time to get to know her. She was so little, like a girl, and so adorable. This was her home, and she didn't live there, we did. You are allowed only one child in China; if you have another, you lose your government job. They have a fourteen-year-old son nicknamed Dino. He doesn't like the New House because it's too far away from the city and he would be bored out here "in the country." We talked for a long time on the deck looking out at the mountains with the pagoda-style firehouse at the top. Below, people on the first floor of the condo have their own individual tiny garden. She asks me about America. Does everyone have huge gardens and yards? She would love to visit in maybe five years when she can retire. She cannot travel now. She only gets one week of vacation a year—her boss decided he does not like to travel or vacation, so no one gets to. The Chinese live under these conditions because they need their jobs. There are too many people—170 million in Beijing. Astounding! Everyone is replaceable many times over. Is she glad she has a son? She wishes she had a daughter. Her son doesn't talk to her. What's new, he's a fourteen-year-old boy? I showed her the pictures of my family—pictures of Page's wedding with both husbands in attendance. Both the Chinese families were very interested in my family. It's the mutual admiration society! Jason, Sandra, Justin, and their cook show up about an hour later. I was dressed to impress with my new red silk jacket, new black silk trimmed capris, and Uggs boots from the black market. I was every bit the 5'10" fashion model with the perfect wig and perfect eye make-up—a vision of happiness and long life. I loved them, and they loved me back.

Noble was cooking like a maniac in the tiny kitchen, sweating and talking with our guests. Jason's cook forcibly takes over the cooking. "These Americans cook too simple," she tells Sandra. Noble can relax now and play with his godson, eighteen-month-old Justin, who is now wearing his gift from Noble—a *Colorado* baseball cap and Robeez leather race car shoes both from Mountain Moppets. I give all the adults their presents, which consist of American antiaging skin care products. They are all so appreciative; they love all things American. I also gave Jason a copy of *The Secret* movie. He already knows it; but I knew he would find it very interesting. We attempted to watch it together, but Jenhua had too many questions for Jason about the meaning of the movie. Jason leaned toward me and said he would watch it later, alone, when he could really listen and understand it. We ate the excellent food that Noble/cook prepared—steamed dumplings, shrimp and vegetables, mushrooms, carrots, and cucumbers sliced so unbelievably thin. For dessert we had kiwi, sliced watermelon, mango, and dark chocolate. Then it was time for everyone to go home. I was completely exhausted in a good way, and so was Noble. We went to bed the minute they walked out the door. We both thought the party was a great success.

Party at the new house

The following days in Beijing were filled with every other day appointments at Dr. Li's and magical adventures on the days in between. I did manage to get my money wired finally, so Noble was happy. I could pay my way with Dr. Li and have some fun at the silk/black market. Jenhua brought me a city bike when we met downtown so he and I could ride through Peking University. That was a beautiful experience, seeing the largest university in China with all its historical buildings and gardens. Jenhua and I always had ice cream together. I loved that sweet, simple intelligent man. He was a geophysicist. He had predicted one of the big earthquakes in China. I was exhausted at the end of that day. It was about that time that Noble started giving me foot rubs every night for about thirty to forty-five minutes before we went to bed depending how long he could last. He would put Burt's Bees body lotion on his beautiful powerful hands and do the equivalent of reflexology on my feet and legs. I loved that time with him because it was the intimacy I craved from him. Those foot rubs were better than an orgasm because I was in pain and it gave me a lot of relief. I would lie on the sofa where I slept, and we would talk about the day and listen to the music I had playing on my computer's iTunes. I could stare at his handsome face and reflect on how lucky I was that he brought me to China and Dr. Li. He was as good as Dr. Li with my feet, and I knew he was giving me the gift of his attention and concern for my well-being. It was sensual. I loved it.

I went to the silk market four times while I was in Beijing. That was my element. After owning Mountain Moppets for more than twenty years, I was a consummate shopper. I had gone to market two or three times a year for all that time. Most of those years I had Sybil to share the experience with. Every time I entered that six-story building on Silk Street in downtown Beijing I was pumped and the angel Sybil was sitting on my shoulder. I felt her presence there, and we had so much fun together! Two of the days, I barely got out of the basement. Some of my favorite tiny boothlike spaces were there literally packed with designer goods. What caught my eye right away were Ralph Lauren cashmere sweaters and boys' toddler clothes, Dolce and Gabana, Uggs boots, Puma tennis shoes, designer silk underwear, and pajamas. My money was disappearing like water. Everything was too good to be true.

After the silk market that day I was taking a cab to meet Noble, Jenhua, Sunyen, and Dino for dinner. They wanted to treat us to Peking duck. *Wow*! Such delicious food we had day and night. Jenhua drove us to the New House and I couldn't wait to show Noble my purchases. Before I could show him, he went outside to have a cigarette. He tells me he started smoking because he's stressed. Why? Is it because of me? He never explains or answers. When he comes back in, I start showing him my goodies. I bought him a silk shirt and sky blue cashmere sweater. He just starts going off on me. "I told you not to buy me anything. I'll just ruin it. You never listen, do you? I don't want it!" "Okay, Noble, I'll just give it to someone else who will appreciate it. You told me you wanted a silk shirt." He grabs that out of my hand and goes to his bedroom. Silence. I didn't get a foot rub that night. I was so pissed off. Who acts like that when someone gives them a gift?

I had a long night—so much pain in my legs. I was surprised because I had very little pain during the marathon-shopping day. I got Noble up in the middle of the night to give me a foot massage. I had tried all my tricks and nothing was helping. Finally I got some relief. I woke up feeling so sad and mad still about last night. I wrote Noble the following e-mail:

Don't you know

Mon, Jun 15, 2009 at 8:29 AM

Noble,Noble,Noble,

I had such a wave of sadness come over me because I can see now that you let this quack doctor convince you that it would be better if you weren't intimate with me on this trip. That has hurt me over and over again these last 6 weeks from you telling me you felt negative about the relationship to you accusing me of being a stalker. What the fuck, Noble. Do you really let people control you like that? You were the most genuine, lovable person I remember and we had such a good time together in Colorado Springs. Even the first few days you were back in Seattle were great. Then you went to see that fucking individual you call a doctor of some sort. Talk about trying to play God. He came into my space and ruined a perfectly wonderful happening. That is such bullshit that you were afraid I was so totally in love with you that you needed to cool it. I'm the prize here,Noble, you are a narcissist. I am a beautiful, sexy,intelligent woman. I deserve way better than this. If you don't respond to this in words or an e-mail, am I to think you are gay or just to depressed to care about sex? When you were in The Springs, you told me you would have had babies with me, that we had a very special relationship together when were young. You also had a very large erection in my bedroom confirming that I do turn you on. Quit lying to yourself and me, Noble. You should be grateful that I care so much about you, because you have been pretty weird ever since I came to Seattle. Who taught you to respond to gift giving the way you do. I can't believe it was your mother. She has more class than that. Was it the shrink again? When you behave like that you sound like a spoiled little boy.

As far as I can see,Noble, my biggest sin is that I enjoy talking, on the phone, to my friends. Why do you think I have so many who love me? It's because I take the time with people to know them and let them know me. The greatest source of joy and happiness in life comes from your relationships with people. You must know that ,don't you?

The next few passages are taken directly from my journal in China:

As always with Noble, life starts all over again in the morning with a new beginning. Don't go back. That's how it should be really. We take the bus to see Dr. Li. I love Dr. Li. He is so cute. He is like a perfect little man. Genius little man. He is filled with happiness and joy, and he wants me to be too. We are practicing English during every session. So far he knows terms related to my pain: *a little, a lot.* He loves it when I say I'm happy. I'm always very happy at the end of my session. He has velvet hands like Noble's. He massages my feet for about forty-five minutes using reflexology, and then does the same with my whole body, looking for the pain in my hip where the pinched nerve is. The pain in my feet and ankles is more from the chemotherapy than from the pinched nerve. I'm detoxing *big-time.* I think if I were at home with no massages, I'd probably be hospitalized for the pain without my Scorpion medicine and the attention of four men (Noble, Jenhua, Dr. Li, and Jason). It's a group effort, and I love them all. Noble made a great dinner. He gave me an incredible foot massage. It's so great. I get to lie on the sofa and stare at him. His hands are beautiful and expressive. He's making love to my feet. Who could ask for more? This home is very tranquil and peaceful. It's all white—wall, floor, and furniture. Any art pops. Of course, if it were mine, I'd bring in lots of color—China red, green, blue. Rugs, overstuffed furniture. Comfort, comfort. Art that means something to me. It could be spectacular. It is spectacular.

June 9

Botanical Gardens: The gardens—pictures speak a thousand words. Noble was a prince—pushed me around in the wheelchair all day. He is so sweet to me and so sexy. Then he had to escape downtown. I was glad to have the time alone. I have the most incredible playlist of songs. I listen to the music for hours and dance to it. It's my new qigong—American style. I think it's the best exercise.

June 10

Dr. Li: My hip is almost completely well. I didn't have any needles in my hip today. Only hands and feet. Pretty good. We rode the bus for hours. I had had enough, and after lunch, I took a cab to the New House. I love the time alone without Noble. He likes to hang out with Jenhua downtown. I'm waiting for the velvet hands to rub my feet.

June 11

Lily-Summer Palace-twelve

Ginny and Lily at Summer Palace

Ginny on Lake

Ginny in wheelchair with calligrapher

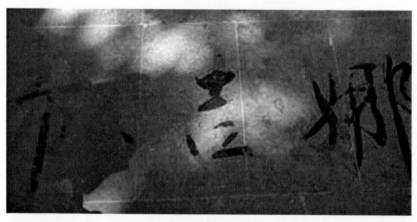

My name Fu Ji Na

I could not sleep this night. I have developed a bad cough from the pollution in Beijing. It's very nagging, and it's not going away. I spent most of the night calling everyone on my Skype contact list. I talked to Ara, Dean, Barbara Stanley, Cami, and Manh. I can't wait to see Manh. He will make me feel alive. I can't stand Noble anymore. He doesn't deserve me. He is really hollow and disconnected from human relationships, especially those between a man and a woman. He has serious intimacy issues. The only person he is intimate with is his mother. How pathetic is that? I know she would never want that to happen to her son, but it has. He will be so alone when I leave. I have given him every opportunity to connect with me. I am so open. I know there are very few people as open and free and happy as I am. He will have a sad life, eventually realizing that happiness is created only from your relationships. How intimate can men be with each other?

June 12

Today I will see Dr. Li and then go to the silk market. That will be fun. I can buy things for people who will appreciate them. Sunday Jenhua and I will go to the Heavenly Temple. So the book will end in a different way. However it ends it will be how it's meant to be. It will be real and genuine. I'm going to have so much fun at the silk market.

After Dr. Li, I told Noble he should fire his pychiatrist who he's had for twenty-five years. It is just ridiculous that he has been trained not to feel highs because they are usually followed by a low. So he is only experiencing flat and lows, and thus, the smoking. That breaks my heart. No one should have to live like that. He needs a psychologist to talk to, not a psychiatrist who prescribes medication. To hell with Western medicine. He should be in a totally different place after twenty-five years. Drugs have changed. Philosophies have changed. I'm not giving up on him yet.

June 13

Noble and Jenhua are out getting me antibiotics and codeine cough medicine—the pollution finally got me. They are also looking for *The Last Emperor* movie and Chinese lanterns from the Star Market. I'm a prima donna still, even though Noble and I really had it out—especially me. He isn't thinking correctly. I'm so outraged! The neurologist who diagnosed me definitively with MS, Dr. Patricia Fodor, and Noble's psychiatrist were trying to play God with both of us. For so long I have believed a thing about myself that isn't true. Fuck them! They should pay! I'm finally feeling better after many, many Chinese candies to suck on, antibiotics, and disgusting cough medicine. What if I didn't have connections? Maybe I could have died—I was that sick. I feel much better now, but so weak. I must have peed twenty times. My swollen ankles are way down. I see Dr. Li tomorrow and maybe I will have to rest one more day. I need another suitcase for all my loot. I have an amazing stash. We will all look smashing at Kaitlyn's wedding.

June 14

Dr. Li told me four times that I am beautiful. He said, "Before needles no, but after needles yes." My happiness must show in my face. I only have two treatments left. I truly believe that will be enough. I will go home completely healed.

We just experienced the biggest thunder and lightning storm on the lanai of the condo. Everything seems bigger in China. The sky came alive with huge thunder claps—I mean *huge*. Scary huge. It rained for a long time—a cleansing rain that could clean the pollution out of the air. I still want to rest and sleep in my red silk pajamas.

Noble went to the store and brought a huge suitcase home for me. It should work perfectly. It's like a duffle bag with a zipper on wheels. He also cooked an excellent dinner of thinly sliced roast beef, tomatoes, and rice noodles on soup. We had green tea that Jenhua gave us as a gift in beautiful tins—one for each of us. All of a sudden I told Noble he was going to miss me when I'm gone. No one to have dinner with and cook for. No one to do things with, ride the bus and subways, download pictures for. No one to give foot massages, no fun conversations to share, no one to plan for.

No one to spoil, no one to worry about, no one to share stories with. He agreed he would miss me by saying, "I probably will." Then I kept going; I couldn't help it. I knew he would eventually shut down, but he hung in there quite a while. I confronted him about the quack psychiatrist who convinced him that it would be better not to be intimate with me, and how that really upset me. How could he let someone have that much power over him? I knew thirty-five years of depression was huge, but did he agree that I had been through an extraordinary amount of heartache and pain in my life? That brought a reaction. He said, "I have told you I agree that you have been through an awful lot." "It's way, way more than you've been through, Noble." "Really, what I've been through is not that much." "I deserve to be happy, Noble, and I am, but you and your quack so-called shrink together concocted this scenario where I was the enemy. How could you let someone have that much influence on you and believe him? Noble, you are a smart, brilliant guy, but you are going the wrong direction here. Noble, I am not the enemy. I adore you. I am so sexually attracted to you. I have chemistry with you. I did the moment I met you, even though I was married to someone else I loved so much. I went back to him because you told me to, and I loved him so much. There was never any question I would go back." Then I broke down about Michael, not Noble. I started to cry feeling that old pain in my heart, thinking about how much he suffers day after day, how no one gave him the recognition he deserves. "Just think what he sacrificed for all of us in Vietnam and how he suffers with PTSD—the flashbacks and the torment he feels every day of his life. It's so unfair. I want to take away his pain. I can't. It just sucks for him." Then I went to bed, took half a Xanax, a cough medicine, and an antibiotic, and slept like a baby.

I woke up crying again about Mike, just uncontrollable weeping. I could not stop. The pain in my heart was palpable. When Noble came out of his bedroom, I let him know I was not crying about him, but Mike. I was finally able to pull myself together and called Chas, and he asked me to show him around the condo. He was really fascinated. I carried my computer around and showed him the high-rises outside from the lanai. Then the gardens down below, where everyone on the first floor had their own personal garden. Then we toured the whole house, and Noble took over while I went to the bathroom. When I came back, I talked to my two incredibly smart and beautiful grandchildren.

This day was my eleventh visit to Dr. Li, and he finished releasing the nerve that had been pinched to some degree or other for twenty-two years. I'm healed! No pain in my hip! Miracles do happen. Jason called. Sandra wanted to pick us up in a taxi and deliver us to a special Korean restaurant for lunch. She and Jason wanted to treat Noble and me, just the two of us, and then Jason would pick us up in his super Audi, and we would all go for a picnic out in the country at a monastery that was a thousand years old. The Korean barbeque was incredibly delicious, cooked right at our table. There must have been seven or eight courses. Our Korean waiter was very attentive and carefully cooked the chicken thighs on the hot grill in the center of our table and then the short ribs and sliced onions. We had four or five dipping sauces for our pleasure. Finally we finished up, and I saw Jason pulling up in front of the huge floor-to-ceiling glass windows we were seated in front of.

The first thing Jason said when we got in the car was to Noble. "Noble, you should listen to Ginny. She is your best critic."

Jason was very enthusiastic and told us the plan for the late afternoon and evening. We would stop at his condo in the Communist complex and pick up Sandra, baby Justin, the nanny, and our picnic, which Sandra had put together. The nanny sat on the floor in the back again. We headed out battling the traffic of Beijing for a while, but soon enough we were on our way toward the country and the mountains. We drove through some beautiful scenery and farms with stands on the side of the road selling fruits and vegetables. I remember the strawberries. Jason gave a running commentary on the history of the people who lived outside of Beijing and slowly started preparing us for the monastery—a thousand years of history. OMG, I could hardly grasp the significance of that. Justin was in the $1,200 stroller from America, and we ascended a series of ancient steps and entered the sanctuary. There were beautiful tables and chairs among the trees, and we were seated in a gorgeous spot near the restaurant, which was very classy and beautifully appointed.

Jason explained that only the higher class Chinese, the wealthy, knew about this place. We settled in, and the waitress brought out a tray with miniature teacups and a pot of oolong tea. Jason explained the significance of the way we drink the tea. First we breathe in the essence and smell of the tea and close our eyes and meditate for a moment. Just being in a place so ancient produced a Zenlike experience. I felt so grateful for my life. I was at peace with myself. It was a beautiful warm evening, and sitting outside in the pristine mountain air was exquisite. Jason and I started talking about how this place would be where we wanted to be when the year 2012 comes and the catastrophe happens. Sandra had packed red cherries, pistachios, almonds, and a few other goodies to snack on. We continued to eat and drink many cups of oolong tea. Then Jason told me how beautiful I was. He asked me if I was this beautiful when I was young. I was feeling a little frustrated with Noble because he wasn't participating in the conversation, so I said, "Ask Noble. He knew me when I was young." So Jason said, "Noble, was Ginny beautiful when she was young?" I couldn't hear exactly what he said, but I think it was, "Yes, she was the most beautiful girl."

Sandra and I got up from the table and started exploring the premises. We began walking on stone steps that were artistically built into the mountain and just went up and up. I had to stop when I got tired and realized I had to walk down. Baby Justin was right there with Sandra.

Noble and I walked through the Tea House Museum, and then it was time to go to the New House because we were all getting tired. We were actually very close to the condo. After we all loaded in the car, it was only about twenty minutes on a new highway to the condo we called the New House. I was leaving the day after tomorrow. What a fabulous ending to my visit in Beijing.

The last morning in Beijing, Noble came out of his bedroom and said, "Ginny, I don't want to have a relationship with you. I don't even want to be friends." After all was said and done, I couldn't even react to that statement. We had to be at my last appointment with Dr. Li at eleven and then go to the airport by two thirty. Jenhua was driving us everywhere with my two huge pieces of luggage filled with 150 lb of cashmere silk, Uggs boots, and jewelry. Dr. Li was his usual happy, happy self, and we got busy right away. This visit was for good measure because he had already released the nerve on the eleventh visit. I simply had no pain after that eleventh appointment except for the neuropathic pain caused by the chemo. That pain is such a nagging pain.

He stuck the needles around Noble's eyes, and I couldn't look anymore; it kind of made me queasy to think about those needles going so close to his eye. It was working little by little, just like my nerve, little by little. Dr. Li and I were in love with each other. Very good doctor, very, very good patient. Dr. Li and I just connected. Little English or a lot of English, he was my man. He released my nerve, so he will always be one of my symbols. Noble got me to him, but we did the work together, Dr. Li and I. We made a superb team. We were both winners. Half an hour of reflexology, half an hour of deep tissue massage, half an hour of needles. He healed me; I was healed. He said, "You beautiful before needles, but after needles you *so* beautiful!" Miracle number two in six months. I am one lucky girl!

Now to the airport. I don't remember if we ate lunch, but knew I would be fed well on the plane back to the United States. We can't compete with that Chinese Hainan Airlines. There were pillows, socks, mango juice, coconut juice, free alcohol, twenty-six different movies, and delicious Chinese food, and I sat next to a spectacular guy, Zack, who wanted to set me up with his uncle who was a Heisman trophy winner. I would have been happy with him. He taught English to a little girl in Tibet.

When we got to the airport, I started to get a little choked up thinking about saying good-bye to Jenhua and Noble. After all, we had all been on this amazing adventure together—Dr. Li, Ginny, Noble, Jenhua, and Jason. I really loved them all so much. They all changed my life in a way that I could have never imagined in my wildest dreams. Noble got a wheelchair for me right away. Everything was going so fast, and we're heading to the place where Jenhua and Noble couldn't go any further. I started to cry, and Jenhua hugged me in the chair. When I turned to Noble, I looked up and saw his arms coming around me. He kissed me on the lips and said, "Ginny, I'm going to miss you."

Now I was alone until I got on the plane and met Zack. He got me to Seattle feeling beautiful, once again with a younger man. The trip back (a twelve-hour flight) was delightful with lots of conversation and movies and even a little sleep. Manh called me on my cell phone. He was waiting for me, and it was about two thirty in the afternoon. I was so happy to see him, and he was all about business. "Come on, let's go. Let's get your luggage, and let's get out of here." Before I knew it I was back in the house with my favorite guy, imagine that. He hauled all my big honkin' luggage inside, and I immediately opened where I thought his presents were. He wanted a silk Chinese-style shirt with the frog-style buttons and a cashmere sweater. I got him a black V-necked Ralf Lauren black label cashmere sweater, for $58. It's $595 in the online catalogue; I checked one night in Beijing on my Mac book computer. Noble did a magnificent job hooking us up in Beijing. We could Skype all my people and call anyone on a Skype phone without a picture almost for free. Then he downloaded all my pictures so I could do a travelogue. He's such an engineer, you just gotta love him.

Manh liked his gifts and that's when I got him to agree to the helmet idea for Griffin's birthday in October. I think I took a nap then. He took me to dinner later at an excellent Mexican restaurant. When we came back to the house, he told me he would take me to the EMP (Experience Music Project) the next day. Hurrah! I took a Xanax and went straight to bed. I hadn't slept in twenty-four hours. I woke up at about ten in the morning and took a few pictures of the coy pond and Teacup, Manh's adorable dog. I made him get up after he begged for fifteen more minutes. "Ginny, you get ready, and I'll go get something to eat for us and then we'll go, okay?" We had baked Kentucky fried chicken. Everything tastes super good to me since my taste buds came back in triplicate. Chemotherapy made everything taste like cardboard. "Let's go, are you ready?

Come on, get in the car. I'll be right there." We go to Park and Ride, Seattle's best in public transportation. We go underground where the subway is because it's Saturday and they let the buses do that. Pretty soon we're at the monorail. What a trip, sitting and seeing all the water and sky above you, and it drops you off in front of the EMP. Wow! Manh looks super hot in his Addidas dark green pants and jacket. He even has a green cover for his iPhone. He's wearing some awesome white tennis shoes, out of his collection of about fifty. That boy doesn't miss a beat.

We enter the EMP, which is a work of art architecturally. Paul Allen had put this amazing museum together to pay tribute to the history of music from the beginning of rock, jazz, and other various genres of music in this century. From the air the EMP looks like a giant guitar all lit up. So cool. Manh goes up to the front desk and manages to get us in for free because he has someone else's pass while the guy is in jail. We ask for a wheelchair because it's a lot of walking for me and we are going to spend a couple hours checking the whole fabulous experience out. I'm so excited. We start with the two-story tree in the main lobby that has hundreds of electric guitars on it. Guitars collected from everyone from Elvis to Eric Clapton, Prince, John Mayer, B. B. King, just on and on in every color, shape, and size. Just magnificent. This place is just so me. Manh is being very systematic in showing me all the exhibits. Right away, I realize this whole place is a celebration of my generation's music: Jimi Hendrix, Janis Joplin, The Rolling Stones, The Beatles, Joni Mitchell, and Sly and the Family Stone. I start a running commentary for Manh, and it is apparent that all the thirty-somethings are listening to me too. I'm the visitor/expert on these musicians because I saw most of them *live* back in my high school and college days.

I was on Dayton's Teen Board representing Edina High School. That meant I was a real fashion model with professional photographers and real runway shows. They always put me in the most outrageous fashions. My body was like Twiggy's—long-legged, tall, and skinny. I had the huge eyes too, and we wore false eyelashes all the time. It was a great time for me, the center of attention always. I thrive on that. I'm a Leo, loving the spotlight all the time. I have the self-confidence to hold an audience thanks to Helen. She thought I hung the moon as long as she was alive. We had a fashion show with the Yardbirds playing an actual concert. I think Eric Clapton was the lead guitar at that time. I didn't know who he was yet. They put up scaffolding, and we modeled while they sang. That was the late 1960s. Go-Go dancers and Twiggy were the height of fashion at that time. I was right in the middle of it and part of it big-time!

I keep my commentary going as we go exhibit to exhibit. Manh said at some point, "You never shut up, do you? You will just go on and on forever, won't you? I'm going to get you drunk tonight, maybe then you'll stop talking." I really love this guy; he just teases me and then indulges me in anything I want to do. He wants to make sure I have a good time. What a precious person he is to me. I keep telling about when I saw The Beatles at Bloomington Stadium where Mall of America is now. I was fourteen years old. I saw the Rolling Stones when I was sixteen at Danceland, the dance pavilion in the amusement park in Minnetonka, Minnesota. We hung out there all the time after I got my driver's license. Mick Jagger was right in front of me on stage. I danced to the Rolling Stones in that small venue. I saw Sly and The Family Stone in the gardens outside the Walker Art Center in Minneapolis. Ritchie Havens was there too. I saw Joe Cocker and Rita Coolidge of *Mad Dogs and Englishmen* fame at a venue in downtown Minneapolis. We were seated right in front of the stage at cocktail tables having cocktails. I must have had a fake ID. I remember I loved slow gin fizzes.

The other treat they had at the EMP that day was a tribute to Jim Henson and the Muppets. There were interactive muppet shows, with all the parents of the little kids going behind a big stage and working the very large muppets/puppets. Manh even went behind the stage and worked the crazy blonde girl muppet. He really got into it. I was in the small audience laughing with the kids at the big people behind the stage. Manh knew a lot about Jim Hensen's other work beside *The Muppets.* He told me about *The Dark Crystal*, his favorite movie of all time. Jim Hensen was the complete genius behind that movie, creating all the puppet characters that seemed to be real creatures in the movie. He told me it was the first movie he ever bought when he was like seven. He told me we were going to watch the movie after we go to the best sushi restaurant in downtown Seattle. Sushi sounds so good to me, my mouth starts watering.

We actually see the Dark Crystal that was used in the movie and some of the incredible costumes that Jim Henson designed. There's a bunch of wild transformers and other cool things, but now I'm thinking about food. I tell Manh that I want to go to the gift shop to get Taylor and Griffin some goodies. They have a lot of cool lunch boxes for kids, and he picks out the cutest, which was a bright green Kermie with skull and crossbones and little pink hearts. So adorable, and Manh picked out the best one for my granddaughter. He really is so spot on with everything. We pick out a soft one for Griffy that has an electric guitar printed on it because he's starting preschool at Ruth Washburn. Then I buy a T-shirt for myself, which says, "Keep on rockin' in a tree world" with birds on a tree on the front. Manh says, "We're gonna take a cab so you don't have to walk so far."

We arrive at the sushi restaurant in a matter of minutes. As we go in, I notice how Zenlike and beautiful it is inside. We are seated at a table with benches on either side, so it's a long table. Manh says, "We're having a bottle of champagne, and I'm getting you drunk." I'm just loving every bit of this, because he is so adorable. Then he asks me if he can order the sushi. He orders a unagi roll, a salmon roll with Copper River salmon from Alaska, and a soft-shell crab roll—all my favorite sushi. We eat edamame and drink champagne and talk. He asked me to relax and not talk so much. Just enjoy the beauty of the space we are in. I love Manh. To me, he's the perfect person for me, only he's twenty-seven and I'm a very young fifty-nine. It could work for me. I have never had better sushi anywhere, not even in Alaska, than that from the restaurant in Seattle. I think Manh makes everything taste better for me. We just ate and ate and finished off the champagne. I picked up the tab because I wanted to. What a magnificent day and night, magical.

We took a cab to the Park and Ride and drove home via the liquor store where he bought more Seattle champagne and a 6-pack of beer and Sun Chips. Now we were going to watch *The Dark Crystal* on blue ray flat-screen TV. What a treat! Manh says, "Go get your pajamas on, and we'll watch together while I get you drunk." He started painting this giant transformer that he brought home from the store earlier. I just stared at this beautiful Cambodian guy while he did his magic on the transformer, painting it black first. Now it was time to snuggle in and watch the movie. From start to finish, it was one of the most fantastic movies I've ever seen. I was just enthralled, and Manh was too, even after having seen it probably a dozen times since he was seven. He was attentively filling my glass even more than his own. I hated to see that movie end, and it was fun to watch Manh turn into a little boy again. Now the movie is over and I think we're going to have to go to bed. I'm leaving in the morning for Colorado Springs. He's drinking can after can of beer and letting me have the champagne, which is barely affecting me. Now he comes out with another movie, *Iron Man* with Robert Downey Jr. He is my favorite male actor by a long shot. I have always loved him, through all the rehab and trials and tribulation, everything. This is his true comeback film, and what a winner of a film that was. Gwyneth Paltrow is the love interest, and I tell Manh, "You know, that's what Page looks like except with Nicole Kidman's nose. Who do you think should play her in the movie version of this book?" Manh says, "I think she should play herself, because she's an original." What an amazing thing to say. "Well then, would you want to play yourself in the movie?" "Yes, I would do that." "Okay then, I'll play myself."

He pops the movie in, and we begin watching. I put my leg up on his lap, and after a while he starts holding both my legs in his lap; it feels so good to have him touching me. This movie is fantastic. I would never have gone to see it in the movie theatres. I'm so glad Manh thought of doing this together. I just love him, his creativity, and animated interest in so many things. He's a turn-on, that's for sure. There is real chemistry there for me; I can feel the energy between us. I am digging this movie, and Robert and Gwyneth's chemistry is better than in most movies. This is the validation of comic book movies. The end credits are finally running, and I'm tired. We need to go to bed. I look over at Manh, and he is slumped down in the couch, sleeping. I look at his beautiful face and those luscious full lips for a long time and then I decide to lean over and kiss him. What happened then was pure ecstasy for me. He opened his eyes and maybe he was dreaming about me, because I felt such pure sexual energy rise up in him, and now I was being kissed back with such passion that I just melted into his arms, which were around me now. This is how kissing should be: sensuous, long, and drawn-out. I think I instinctively put my tongue in his ear, which got an amazing response. We were pressing our bodies together, and I was *extremely* turned on. He was delicious.

Then Manh said, "I really have to pee!" So did I. We both got up simultaneously and rushed to the bathrooms at opposite ends of the house. I yelled, "I'll meet you in my bedroom." I peed and went into my bedroom. Almost immediately Manh showed up. He said, "I can't believe you're seducing me. We can't do this." "Yes, we can. Just let go. Just let go, Manh." "Okay, but I'm not doing this in your bedroom. We're doing it in my bedroom." He takes my hand, and we go to his awesome bedroom. It is filled with his art. Custom football helmets line a shelf at the foot of his bed, framed baseball jerseys are hung on the walls, and boxes and boxes of expensive tennis shoes are stacked in neat towers against the wall. He has popped another beer, and then we go at it. Major sensuous kissing, and he tells me he digs the ear thing. He's pulling off my pajama bottoms and his pants. He's all over my body, just doing all the right things, even biting me a few times. This guy is a lover deluxe. We play and make love for a long time, and when he's exhausted, he falls down beside the bed because he is pretty wasted from all the beer. He puts on his knit Fruit of the Loom or whatever boxer shorts. Then I say, "I think I want to put my pajama bottoms on." "Oh no, I want you naked in my bed." It turns me on even that he said that. We do some more kissing, and then he falls into a deep sleep. Eventually I do put my pajamas on and remain in a pseudo sleeplike state until it gets bright outside.

I have to get crackin' because my flight leaves about ten thirty. I have to wake up the lover boy, and he isn't responding very well. Hangover. "Manh you have to help me close my bags." They are so packed with cashmere, silk everything, Uggs boots, jewelry, and other treats for my grandkids that I can't even come close to doing it myself. Now he's up and giving me directions on how to make this happen. "Go out to the car. I'll get all the luggage. We'll be fine." "Manh, you are a good lover." "Thank you." I smile at him. We're on our way to the Sea-Tac Airport, and he pulls up to the drive-through window at Wendy's. We order coffee and breakfast muffins and then we're on our way. I think we're cutting it pretty close. Now we're at the airport in front of the Frontier Airlines door. "I can't go in with you. They will ticket me, so I'm going to load up your luggage on this big cart and push you through the door. Then you're on your own. Bye." I grab a kiss and off I go. I am so going to miss that boy/man. What a giver he is. I will always love him and have him in my thoughts. He is so special. What a great time we had together. That's mine to keep.

Disaster strikes. They won't let me get on the flight. I'm so pissed off. They are giving someone at the gate my ticket. The flight is overbooked. What a fucked up airline. They did one thing right. My luggage was $190 worth of charges over the limit. They give me a pass on that. I'm *lucky* you know. So now I wait two and a half hours for the next flight to Denver. I'm on standby because it's oversold, but I make it on. I'm *lucky*. Arriving in Denver is a relief, and I decide to just call Page and ask her to please drive up to Denver to pick me up instead of waiting for my flight. I can't wait to see her and talk to her about Taylor and Griffin and just be back home to my adorable house in Colorado Springs. It's time to be home again. Before I know it, she is pulling up outside, and we kiss and hug each other and load my unbelievably heavy luggage and head on out of the airport. It's great to be home. I'm ready to sleep in my own bed.

I have Herceptin in the morning at ten. I see Dr. John at nine. He's so cute and enthusiastic. I brought my computer so I could show him the pictures. He looked at all of them because he was genuinely interested. I love Dr. John. I don't much care about seeing Dr. Hoyer because his energy is neglible. Everything is happiness for me. Now I get to go see the angel nurses in the infusion room. I have small presents for all of them—hand-painted chopsticks in a little silk case. They can pick their color. They're a big hit with everyone. I love every one of those angel girls. I even got a call from Brownie, the ninety-two-year-old volunteer who says her secret to longevity is that she didn't worry too much. That's it, one of the secrets: don't worry too much and you'll live longer.

Now all my attention can turn to Kaitlyn's wedding in Durango. We're leaving on Friday and need to be there for the rehearsal at five. Taylor and Griffin are both in the wedding just like in Christine's. Kaitlyn and Christine are Chas's two younger sisters who got married six months apart. We take my Lexus so it's a comfortable ride. The drive to Durango through Alamosa is spectacular. I've always known Colorado is the most beautiful state. This year is the most beautiful I have seen it in a long time. We are definitely out of the drought. Heading up Wolf Creek Pass, I felt like I was in the Heavenly Temple of nature that I saw in architecture in Beijing. The wedding is going to be beautiful and fun. We'll all be dressed from China. Taylor and Griffin look adorable. Picture this. Griffin has on light khaki-colored microfiber pants, a traditional button down collared shirt with the sleeves rolled up twice, not tucked in, and camo tennis shoes. To die for. Then Taylor has a beautiful simple white dress with a wide brown satin sash wrapped around about three times. Of course, they steal the show at the wedding. That wedding was one of the most beautiful weddings I've ever been to. The chapel was all glass and up on a hill, and with the backdrop of the green, green San Juan Mountains, it really was spectacular. I was so grateful to be alive and so grateful for my healing. Two miracles in six months change a person in profound ways. I felt so full to the brim of life. Later, after the ceremony, I heard Taylor was playing on the rocks around the rim of Durango, and a guy who was having a smoke said, "Taylor, you need to get away from those rocks. They're very dangerous." She said, "So is smoking." She's five. Then after the reception started, she and I went to the bathroom together, and when she came out, she bent over on a chair and said, "Oh, Gigi, I have such a bad stomach ache. They must have put high fructose corn syrup in the wedding cake!" She's five.

I was really into dancing at the reception. There was a great DJ who led the whole reception as far as announcing the time for toasting and dinner buffet by table. It was very organized and well thought out, except for one thing: they didn't allow enough time for toasting in my opinion. Christine, the sister of the bride, led off the toasting. She was funny and a bit long, but then the best man came forward and gave a shorter toast. The father of the groom came forward then, and the DJ almost cut him off. This man was one of the most elegant and handsome Mexican men I have ever met, just pure class. He gave a very emotional toast with tears, telling this beautiful newly married couple to be good to each other and never go to bed mad at each other. It was a killer really. I thought I could be the perfect comic relief with a toast about how I went all the way to China to get their wedding gift, but as I started walking up to the microphone, I was told the toasting was all over by my daughter, Page, and to go sit down, this wasn't about me. Just sit down. I have to say that stung a bit. I wasn't trying to make it about me; I was trying to make it about them, Kaitlyn and Tom. I was a little miffed, but I decided to suck it up. After a little while, I went downstairs to the bar and ordered a bottle of champagne to share with anyone who wanted to toast with me. It ended up being a lot of wonderful women of all ages. They were all interested in my stories about China, which inevitably lead to the miracle stories. People are always amazed and inspired by my life. I'm always promoting my book. Everyone is so interested; many take out a pen and paper and write the title and my name down, Virginia Wesley.

After a lot of conversation, I decided to go upstairs to see if we could get people up and dancing. I went up to the DJ and said, "No one is dancing. Why don't you play some Michael Jackson. Everyone my age will get up and dance to the king. You can't sit still if Michael Jackson is singing." Of course, that started everything moving. We were all up on the dance floor, and I just danced with all the folks my age, which was most of us at the wedding. Then all the young people came upstairs from the bar, and we had a giant danceathon. Taylor immediately came to dance with me. She is just a beautiful and precious five-year-old who embraces her beauty and enhances it by being spontaneous and performing in front of people whenever she gets the chance. She and I actually had a duet performance when all eyes were actually on us while she danced around me in a very dramatic fashion. I wish someone had it on film because it was really quite beautiful the way she moved around me. Many people commented on it afterward.

When the music reached a crescendo, I saw that Steven, Chas's younger bother, and his friend Dalton were just sitting around looking bored, so I coaxed them to get up and dance with me. Both of those boys can dance, but Steven is beyond good, he is an awesome dancer. I try to imitate his moves because he is so original; that's it—he's just an original. I love Steven; he always helped me when I was really sick and depressed. He would walk me to my car after Thanksgiving and Christmas celebrations at Leigh's house. He and Chas are very handsome brothers. Kaitlyn and Christine are beautiful sisters. Definitely some good genes there. Their father deserted the family when Chas was seventeen. It's very hard to understand how a man could leave four such beautiful children. Leigh has done an amazing job raising all those kids by herself. It really has been a whole family effort with Leigh's mother, Florence, at the head of the family and then Uncle Robbie and Aunts Gayle and Moina. They are really an incredible family with everyone supporting each other.

We all retired to the General Palmer Hotel after leaving the reception. All five of us were sharing a room in this very lovely Victorian hotel. It was quite plush really, with beautifully appointed rooms and lobby. I got to sleep in a queen-sized bed with Taylor and Griffin. What a blast to sleep with my grandkids! Griffin tends to be the destroyer at age two, so I had to separate them eventually so we could all go to sleep. He slept like the baby he still is with my arms wrapped around him most of the night. He is such a beautiful kid that in the morning I tried to wake him up with hugs and kisses. He is just irresistible.

Taylor and I got up and went to the breakfast area downstairs in our robes and jammies and let Page and Chas and Griffin sleep in. When they were all ready, we went across the street to have great Mexican food and do a little shopping. I bought an incredible high-fashion down jacket on sale with beaver trim on the hood. I'm going to wear it when I start skiing again this winter after a ten-year forced hiatus. I quit skiing when I couldn't get up when I fell. The muscle in my leg was already atrophying.

We packed up the car and headed for Alamosa to see Mike and Mackie's spread. Page had always told me I would hate it there. I was totally blown away when we pulled up in their driveway and I saw where they actually lived. Spectacular! They are totally surrounded by two mountain ranges, The San Juans and the Sangre de Cristos, 360 degrees, just like the name of my past venture boutique in Colorado Springs. There was the guesthouse that I had heard so much about. It had just had the trim painted red to match the corrugated roof. It was so close to the main house that it almost seemed part of it. We entered the main house, and I found it to be very cozy, but wide open with saultillo tiles throughout so Michael could twirl around freely in his wheelchair. Mike has his own huge wheelchair-accessible bathroom that he can just wheel into without any problems, not like when we were married and the bathrooms were all such a struggle. The last house we lived in together had a beautiful bathroom, but he lived there only a few months. That was at the end when he left me for the last time.

Mackie has her own soaking tub with a big window so she can look out at the mountains. She had made fresh rhubarb cobbler for all of us to share at their dinning room table. She looked beautiful with a long skirt and fun, funky cowboy hat. Her skin was glowing; I asked her what she was using, and she said, "Olive oil and Arbonne." She made whipped cream to put on the cobbler, and then we all sat down to eat the warm, yummy delicacy. I was looking down at the knotty pine dining table and realized there was inlaid turquoise in all the knots. Wow! Everything about the place was unusual and special. I was so impressed. Then everybody got up and went outside leaving Mike and me alone in the kitchen. I had told both Mike and Mackie that I wanted to read the dedication of this book to them. Now Mackie was not there, so I went ahead and read it to Michael. I knew I couldn't read it without crying, but I had to do it anyway. Just like I had to call him a few years ago and tell him how much I have always loved him and was so, so sorry about what happened to him, falling off the roof and all. I told him how sad I was that he had to suffer so much and that I just really won't ever get over him and I just wanted to be sure he knew that in case I died before him or something else happened. He just put his head down and then looked up and said he didn't know what to say. Then I asked him if I had the facts straight that he was the only survivor out of his platoon. Then he explained to me what a platoon was. First there are two troops in a company. In each troop there were four platoons, three ground troops with armored personal carriers or tanks and the fourth platoon was air support. As a platoon leader, Mike was the radio guy. He could call in air support whenever he thought it was necessary. He was twenty years old and responsible for fifty-one guys. Some were out on R & R, and some were injured, but as far as he knew he was the only survivor that day. When he was blown off the tank, he had the radio on him and was able to call for help. He was bleeding profusely. The helicopter came in under hostile fire and saved him. They stripped off all his clothes because they couldn't be sure where the blood was coming from—there was so much. The medic asked, "Do you smoke, soldier?" When Mike answered yes, he put a lit cigarette in his mouth, and then Mike got sick. They pulled him up into the copter and flew him off to safety and surgery in Japan. That was my first tragedy and my first miracle.

Now Mike said, "Come on, let's go outside so I can show you around the place." We went out together, and the first thing I noticed was the five white albino turkeys. I had a camera in my hands, and they seemed to know I wanted their picture because they all fanned out at the same time, three in the back, two in the front, picture ready. Unfortunately I didn't get the picture because I was out of room on the digital camera Noble had given me in China. I walked around with my cane, and he was wheeling in front of me; then Page and our beautiful grandkids joined us, forever keeping us joined together as parents and grandparents. There was a peace about this place that I felt as I was viewing the organic vegetable gardens and the amazing geodesic greenhouse that was the home of all the medical marijuana plants. It was all very orderly and well planned. I could see a llama and an alpaca behind a fence. It was getting time to go, so we all loaded in the car. Chas started backing the car out of the driveway, and I had the picture of Mackie and Mike looking content and at peace. It made me happy to have that image to leave with.

That picture snapped out of my mind pretty quickly because I remembered that Page had always said, "You would hate Dad's place, Mom." I loved his place now that I finally was able to see it. It was beautiful and spectacular. Now I was angry with her. At that point Chas said, "In Page's defense, they have fixed it up quite a lot since all Mackie's boys have left. It hasn't always been this nice." That was good of Chas to diffuse my anger. We continued our journey back to Colorado Springs with little to distract us except the kids who are always adorable, especially when they have fallen asleep after a long fun day.

My life resumed after the wedding to its normal pace, and I set my sights on finding my dream car. I had talked to Chas quite a bit about the car I wanted. He was more than happy to help me with it because the car was an Audi A4 Cabriolet convertible. My son-in-law, Chas, is an Audi aficionado, and he had already looked on the Internet to check prices and availability. He assured me there was no problem getting what I wanted—a China red one, a preowned one.

Page stopped over the day after we got back from Durango and started up a conversation with me about her concern that she thinks I'm manic. This disturbs me very much because I know I am just superhappy and she is misconstruing it to be mania. To me that is just a ridiculous notion, and it pisses me off that I have to defend my happiness.

She wants me to see a psychiatrist. I say absolutely not. Then she says, at the very least a psychologist. It starts to get downright nasty, and out of frustration, I tell her that I could see Kirsten Akse. She should schedule the appointment. Kirsten helped me when Page was robbed at gunpoint in Denver and then ended up in the hospital a dozen times over the next two years. That one almost destroyed me. I thought she might die because she lost so much weight. It was like reliving her childhood when we almost lost her.

Page is a person who has been blessed with many lives, like a cat. She definitely is a survivor. We all are, as it turns out. Mike and Page and I have all been given a second chance more than once. I think I have figured out that we are all *lucky*. Being lucky is a very real concept for anyone who is a Buddhist in their philosophy on life, like I am. Except I don't worship Buddha. I don't believe in worshipping any one god. I embrace the right for all people to believe what they want. I respect people's belief in their own personal spirituality; I just don't want them to disrespect mine by trying to convince me their religion is the only true religion of god. Oprah said it best when she said there are many paths to God. That's what I believe.

After having spent five weeks in China, I definitely came to know that I love the basic concepts of Chinese Buddhism. The words that describe it are like music to my ears: longevity, wealth, love, virtue, fame, happiness, luck, heavenly, transcendence, benevolence. When we were in the gift shop at the Great Wall where I bought my jade bracelet, I found some cards in Chinese calligraphy that had the meaning of names on them. I found my name, Virginia. *Fu Ji Na* in Chinese. It means *Whisk Lucky Pretty*. Pretty Lucky Whisk. That's when I realized that I really am a whisk, always stirring things up. Sometimes it gets me in trouble, but mostly I love the excitement I create in my life. I think most people love that about me; they love the excitement too. That's how I know who my people are, if they appreciate that about me. Emotions are contagious, and so is laughter. I have plenty of both of those. I have always been able to sell myself to achieve success. I am selling my enthusiasm and passion; it's genuine.

So Page dropped the ball about making an appointment with Kirsten. Because she did not follow through, I ended up in lockdown at Memorial Hospital in Colorado Springs. This is how it began. I went to see Taylor's summer drama camp rehearsal on a Thursday before the Friday of the performance for the parents. Birgitta De Pree of the Manitou Art Theatre, MAT, was teaching the group of six- and seven-year-olds, and it was centered around the concept of building a spaceship. Taylor was only five, but she was allowed into the class.

I was bathing in the sunshine of watching my little granddaughter interact with the other kids and Birgitta and the student helper. There is nothing so sweet as loving your grandchild and feeling so proud of their every little move as they navigate their way through life. In Taylor's case, it is a magical life because of the parents she has. My daughter, Page, is a gifted artist coming into her own and sharing all her knowledge with Taylor. Her father, Chas, is a loving dad with many talents of his own, and he is still a kid at heart. His own father deserted his family when Chas was seventeen. It seems as though he will not let that loss affect the way he fathers. He is a very loving and responsible dad.

I observed that Taylor was well loved in the class and somewhat reserved, but an enthusiastic participant. Her job was to design the bathroom in the spaceship. I wasn't surprised when I saw it was fanciful and feminine and dramatic just like she is. Sometimes we call her the drama queen. She has joined the club of Royalty just like a lot of little girls her age. She is very emotional just like her Gigi. Page wasn't so emotional when she was that age. I think she learned to be a little tougher because of what she went through before she turned five.

After the rehearsal, I spoke with Birgitta a little and told her how impressed I was with the quality of the theatre and how fortunate we all are to have this community theatre in Colorado Springs. Birgitta and her husband, Jim Jackson, are the award-winning artistic directors of MAT, and well, they should be. The lineup of talent they have put together is truly remarkable for any community. The MAT has enriched so many lives in the Colorado Springs, and there is excellence associated with every performance I have seen there.

Now it's past noon, and all the children have been picked up except Taylor. She and I wait in my car awhile, and then I start to think about how fun it would be to have lunch with her. Chas is running late I guess, but it's fine because I will just call Page and tell her I have Taylor. I ring Page, and she answers; I tell her that I have Taylor and will feed her lunch. Then Page says, "Mom, do not leave with Taylor. Chas will freak out if he gets there and

Taylor is gone." I say, "Okay fine, I will wait until he shows up." Just at that moment Chas pulls up with a big hello and a smile on his handsome face. "Hi, Chas, let's go to lunch. I'll treat, okay?" He asks where I want to go, and I say, "Let's go sit on the patio at Rustica Pizza in Old Colorado City." No, Chas doesn't like that idea. "How about Panera Bread?" I don't like that idea because it's way on the other side of town. He says he kind of wants to feed the kids peanut butter and jelly sandwiches. *What?* "Well then, let's go to Mountain Mama's where we can get organic p and j's." He says that would be good because he needs to shop anyway. So do I. Agreed. "I'll follow you, okay?"

Chas pulls up to the stop light on Twenty-first Street, and I see he's turning left, but I want to go right so I can pick up a dress at Barracuda Bazaar. You know the rest of the story because that's how this book started.

The following week after I was in lockdown at Memorial Hospital was filled with the most ridiculous series of events imaginable. I made an appointment with Kirsten as I promised to do when I was released from the hospital. When I called her and explained the ordeal, she was blown away and very excited to see me. We agreed to meet on the following Monday at one thirty. I had the whole weekend to rest and relax. I needed that time to myself.

Monday came soon enough, but I was ready for my appointment and to get this whole thing behind me. Piece of cake, right? Wrong! I walked into Kirsten's office wearing the new dress I purchased at Barracuda Bazaar, and leggings and Uggs boots from China. I had my cute China girl wig on and was looking like the fashion model I want to be. Kirsten was pacing across her office lobby talking on her cell phone while I was sitting there. Finally after what I felt was too long a wait, she called me into her office. I seated myself on her comfortable couch and immediately started talking. She interrupted me and said, "Before you start, Ginny, I have to tell you I did speak to your sister-in-law and your daughter last night, and I do believe you are manic." I flushed all over because that was the last thing I expected to come out of her mouth. I said, "Kirsten, I'm so disappointed in you." "I knew you would be." Then began a conversation between the two of us about mania. She said I absolutely had mania, and I would say no, happiness. Back and forth mania, no happiness, mania, no extreme happiness. Then she said she wouldn't treat me if I didn't agree to see a psychiatrist and get on medication. Absolutely not! Round and round we went until she told me that if I saw an Eastern doctor who treated mania, she might agree to that. "Kirsten, that would be an acupuncturist, and there is no such word in their vocabulary as mania. They might treat it with herbal tea and massage." Just then my friend Sharon called me on my cell phone, and I decided to take the call. "Hi, Ginny, what are you doing?" "Well, I'm at the psychologist's office, and she wants me to see a psychiatrist and get on medication." "Ginny, you stand up and walk out of her office right now." That's exactly what I did while Kirsten was looking for insurance forms. The last thing she said to me was, "I suppose you don't think you should pay for this visit?" I was happy to say no. As I walked out the front door, I wanted to dance and laugh and yell, "I'm free."

The next day, I was invited to lunch with Daryl, the man who bought my building, the Mountain Moppets building. We were going to discuss the possibility of him buying me out of the mortgage he owed me in payments for a discount. He picked me up at my house, and we went to Pizzeria Rustica across from Mountain Moppets and sat on the patio. It was another perfectly beautiful day in Colorado Springs. I never get over what a beautiful place I live in. I could see Pike's Peak off in the distance as we were entering the restaurant. We were seated on the patio and decided to split a pizza and a salad. Daryl and I were discussing the possibilities of a buyout. About halfway through lunch my cell rang. It was Dr. Hoyer, my oncologist. Why was he calling in the middle of my lunch? "Hi, Ginny." "Dr. Hoyer, why are you calling me? Aren't you busy with your patients?" "Well, I'm thinking you need a complete psychiatric evaluation at Cedar Springs Hospital." "Oh no, Dr. Hoyer, now you have crossed the line. You are completely out of your realm of expertise here. You are an oncologist, not a psychologist." "Well, I think you may be experiencing mania." "Listen, Dr. Hoyer, I am experiencing happiness, and you are totally out of line here. I don't want to be like you. You have a limp handshake, and you are like a funeral parlor director. I want enthusiasm, and you are boring. I need to have an oncologist who brings me up, not down. I think I need a different oncologist." "I didn't know you felt that way about me. I could withhold your Herceptin, you know." "Fine. I don't want it anyway. I don't need it. It costs $10,000 dollars every three weeks, and it's just a pass-through drug because I don't have cancer. I'm a medical miracle, remember? I'm your claim to fame! I'm going to hang up now, Dr. Hoyer, because you are treading on dangerous ground." I was so flabbergasted and started to tell Daryl what was going on when my cell rang again. It was Page. "Mom, I'm at your house cleaning out your car because of the mess Griffin and Taylor made from the wedding, and there is a police car pulling up in front of your driveway. I have nothing to do with this! Where are you?" At that point I said, "Page, I'm out of here. Call me later!" I wasn't sure what my rights were after the hospital scene, so I told Daryl we needed to finish up fast and drive me to my friend Melanie's house in Manitou Springs where I felt I would be safe. We hightailed it out of there, and he delivered me to Melanie and her wise advice safe and sound.

Melanie is a friend I have acquired since my cancer treatment, and what an amazing acquisition it has been! She is a beautiful girl inside and out, and when I met her at the drug dispensary in the basement of the Cancer Center of Memorial Hospital she had a knockout red wig on. She told me that she got it for free at the hospital and it was from the Rachel Welch collection. She was quite the fashion plate like me, and we bonded immediately. When I walked in her door, she was waiting for me with an invitation to sit down at her kitchen table and have a glass of iced tea. That led to some great conversation about my current situation and laughter about how ridiculous it was. We laughed hard, and then she asked if I would like to share a bowl. I said sure I would, even though I hadn't smoked pot for many years. She was so charming and so intelligent. She reminded me of the female counterpart to my first husband, Mike, except without the anger and rage. She just knew way more information than it was possible for one human being to know. It was like she was tapping into the race memory, the collective memory of mankind. That's what Mike does. We've joked about it for years, but I really believe that's what they are doing.

Talking about her connection to the American Indian brought on an invitation from her to read my totem animals. I enthusiastically agreed. She produced a deck of cards and a book. She explained that I would choose my own seven cards from the fanned out shuffled deck. This reading introduced me to a whole new way of viewing the meaning of my life through the animals on the planet we walk through life with. Here's how my reading went:

Introduction by Melanie

My east animal, spider

East is also known as the Golden Door or Gateway Animal. Spider invented the art of writing and weaving the first alphabet. Her symbol is 8, the shape of the spider meaning infinite possibilities. She weaves the web of fate—change can happen at any time. Female creator that weaves the patterns of life. Expansiveness.

My south animal, raven

Protects my inner child. *Magic.* Courage to enter darkness of the Void—The Great Mystery and deep meditative states. I have earned the right to see a little more. Black—the seeking of answers, changing form and shape. *Raven* guides the change in consciousness. New reality and dispels disease. Carries all energy flows. The power of the unknown. Further enhance my growth. Carry an intention or healing energy, thought, message, call upon *raven*.

My west animal, armadillo

Leads me to my own personal truth and inner answers. *Boundries.* Armadillo on the back. Gift—harmful intention or words roll off. Make a circle. Within the circle include desires, joys, what I am, and what my will is—unconscious. *Define my space.* Giving back sense of self.

185

My south animal, otter

Balancing, staying grounded. Women medicine. Otter skins were used for medicine bags. *Playful.* Earth and water. Personification, adventuresome. Beauty of the balance of the female side. Creates space for others. *Sisterhood.* Expresses joy for others. Freeness of love without jealousy. Shares the bounty of life with others.

My north animal, black panther

[Melanie told me she never had seen anyone draw the black panther.]

Embracing the *unknown.* Knows when to speak and when to listen. *Color black*—seeking, finding answers, finding truth. Tracks the unfamiliar territory. *Courage.* Helps let go of fears. *Goes with the flow.* Leaping empty handed into the void with implicit trust.

My above animal, ant

Patience. The guardian of our dreams knows about victory at the end of the line. Slowly and deliberately eats. Trusts in the universe to provide. *Good of the whole.*

My within animal, snake

This is the most important card because it is within you and also surrounds you.

Transmutation. Hearts joy—faithful to own truths—protects my sacred place. Enter my space by invitation only. Sexuality, psychic energy, immortality. Snake people are very rare. Transmute all poisons—[Did I do that with the chemotherapy?] Knowledge that all things can be transmuted. Understanding and acceptance of male and female energies inside me.

Passion
Procreation
Wisdom
Intellect
Magic
Leadership

You also get to pick two more animals that walk by your side through life without drawing cards. You can pick from the list in the book or choose from all the animals you personally love. I picked *eagle* and *hummingbird.*

Eagle

Spirit reconnect with the element of air—your higher mind. Creative force. Give myself permission to legalize freedom and follow the joy of my heart's desire. Cocreate with the divine—connect with the divine. Broaden my sense of self. Gather your courage and fly above the mundane.

Hummingbird

Joy. Conjures love. You love life and its joys. Presence brings joy to others. Help others taste the wonders of life. *Laugh* and enjoy the *magic* of *living!*

After the reading, Page called to tell me the police had left and said they would not come back and I should feel free and safe to come home. I was ready to come home and feel safe. Mel drove me home late in the day. Life was so sweet to me.

The following morning I was all showered and dressed and ready to leave my house when the phone rang. It was about 11:00 a.m. "Ginny, this is Dr. Hoyer." "Dr. Hoyer, don't say anything unless it's positive!" He went ahead anyway and said, "I'm thinking of ordering an MRI." "That's a neurological test, Dr. Hoyer. You don't believe what happened in China. You don't believe in Eastern medicine, do you? You think I still have MS, don't you? Who's going to pay for that, Dr. Hoyer? My insurance only covers 100 percent on cancer, not neurological tests." "Well, I was thinking about putting it under the guise of metastases in the brain." "Oh my god, Dr. Hoyer, I can't believe you said that word in front of me, metastases. Now I have to work really hard to put that word in a bubble and make it float away out of my consciousness. You are talking about insurance fraud now. Ordering one test for another. I'm firing you now. Don't ever call me again!" Click, I hung up the phone.

Dr. Hoyer did withhold my Herceptin. I did not receive it for nine weeks. I should have had it every three weeks. It took that long to arrange for another oncologist. It was worth the wait though because I love my new oncologist. He is open to the science of Eastern medicine. His name is Dr. Murphy and is at Rocky Mountain Treatment Center. Dr. Hoyer was not open to Eastern medicine. He was trained at the Mayo Clinic. They are not open. I had a bad experience at the Mayo Clinic in Rochester, Minnesota, once before with Page, remember?

Road Trip across America

I found my dream car after looking at forty-five preowned Audi Web sites on the Internet. I found it on the forty-fourth in Naples, Florida, where Noble's mother lives. I called her and told her most of the story about Noble and me in China. I told her I spent six weeks with her never-been-married son. She was absolutely charming and precious on the phone with me. She insisted I stay the night with her when I flew in to pick up the car. I agreed hoping it would work out for both of us. I really wanted to meet her.

It didn't work out because she called me a few days later and said she had made it into a golf tournament with her girlfriends—a big one at Sawgrass. She would be at the tournament when I arrived. It worked out better for me because after Peter from the Mercedes dealer picked me up at the airport and we finished the paperwork, I had enough time to drive to Sarasota where my dear friend, Lynette from Crested Butte, anxiously awaited me. I left the Mercedes dealership feeling like a million bucks in my Audi A4 Cabriolet China blue convertible. That car is a high-performance one in every way with a kick-ass stereo, and I was so happy it was mine.

Lynette and I connected like the old soul mates we were. I stayed there three days. We reminisced about our lives together and apart, drove around with the convertible top down, went to Siesta Beach, ate delicious seafood, and laughed until we cried. Her daughter, Quana, was there too. She was Page's best friend growing up in Crested Butte, along with Stacy, Sybil's daughter. We talked about how beautiful Sybil was and celebrated her life with a toast, hardly believing she was really gone.

Before I left, I discovered that my journal was missing. It was the strangest thing. This was my journal with my entire trip to China and the journal I kept after Mike fell off the roof and we went to rehab in Minneapolis. I never panicked, but we never found it before I left. I was determined to be okay no matter what happened. I had written a phone number in it before I went to bed, and I thought I left it on the table next to the bed. There was an alarm system in the house, so I knew that if I walked in my sleep and tried to go outside, it would have set the alarm off. Lynette and I pretty much tore the bedroom apart to no avail. We took a break and had breakfast. Then we looked in all the cupboards and the refrigerator. Nothing. Finally Lynette said her journal was missing too. We decided our angels were playing tricks on us and went to the beach. It was a glorious day. I will never forget that sugar sand and the warm ocean water lapping against my feet with my arm around my dear friend Lynette.

Lynette and me at Siesta Beach in Sarasota

My New Dream Car

I bid Quana and Lynette farewell and was sure I could write the book without my journal. I really didn't think it would show up.

My next stop was Gainesville and then Savannah. I had fried chicken, mashed potatoes and gravy, and chocolate pecan pie at the charming bus station there. I took the amazing bus tour of the historic home of one of my favorite books, *Midnight in the Garden of Good and Evil*. I loved the movie too with Kevin Spacey. The tour guide was named Sparky and had been misdiagnosed for nine years with MS too. She had a pinched nerve in her neck. She gave us an unforgettable tour of all the town squares in downtown Savannah.

I got back in my car after the tour and drove to Barnesville, Georgia, where my friend Annie lives. She wasn't there because she was on a trip. She's a flight attendant for Delta/Northwest. I was able to see her beautiful historical Victorian house because her handyman, Whyley, was there working. He gave me a tour and explained a lot about the original fixtures and history of this one remarkable street in the charming Georgia town. Whyley was charming as well. I spent the night there and then headed out the next morning for an eight-hour drive to Chicago.

I was thinking a lot about Noble, but I found my mind going more to Manh. I would talk to them both out loud in the car while I had my six CDs cranked up. I listened to those six artists for the entire trip. I never turned on the radio. My music repertoire was Annie Lennox, my personal diva; Damian Marley; Ziggy's younger brother, Carlos Santana; Tracey Chapman; Steve Barta; and Andrea Bocelli. It was a perfect mix. I got so into the music that I lost track of where I was. My AAA road book was useless. The print was too small, and I couldn't turn the pages while I was driving. The road signs in the south were very different from Colorado, where there are basically two main freeways, I-70 and I-25. Every sign seemed to have four or five different numbers all piled on top of each other. I started noticing the incredible foliage on the left side of the curvy road. All the trees looked like giant topiaries of people and animals. I was tripping on a natural high. I had the thought that cancer patients could heal themselves here because the air was superoxygenated. It was so green and verdant. There was a river on the right side with rafters bobbing down one after another. I was in paradise. I had been driving for eight hours, and I was no closer to Chicago than when I started—I found out that I had just driven through the Great Smokey Mountains of Tennessee. I don't know where I made the wrong turn, but I'm sure glad I did. That windy curvy drive was one of the most beautiful experiences of my spectacular road trip across America.

I drove another two hours and decided I should call it quits in Chattanooga. My cousins in Chicago couldn't believe I was still so far away when I called them. I promised I would be there the next day. They didn't think I could make it in one day. I did it, but it took me from 9:00 a.m. to midnight when I finally got to the outskirts of Chicago under a pouring rain. They drove out to meet me because they were worried about the neighborhood at that hour of the night. I stayed up another few hours talking to my cousin Barbara and her husband Bob. Barbara's mother was my dad's twin sister. We hardly ever saw each other. Her mother and my mother were best friends. I love her even though she is a staunch Republican and we learned we couldn't discuss politics. I left their house at 9:00 a.m. and drove straight through to Minneapolis where a big party was being held for me at 7:00 p.m. What a marathon! I loved it.

I was staying at Mark's house. I love Mark. I had three days of rest in Minneapolis. I fell in love with Mark's beautiful little angel girls, O'Neil and Mave. They are the same age as Taylor and Griffin. In his case, better late than never. It was in Minneapolis that I realized I was finally over Noble. I sent him the following e-mail from Mark's computer.

Done with you

Ginny Wesley <ginny.wesley@gmail.com>   Tue, Jul 28, 2009 at 7:14 AM
To: Noble Irving

Hi Noble,
My road trip has continued to be one miracle after another. I'm at Mark's mansion in Minneapolis and headed to Rapid City to see Mary Harmon/Bartron. I talked to Manh and he said you are staying longer in China, he thinks. I'm so over you,Noble, after the way you have treated me since I left China, like I'm invisible, not even special enough to get 1 e-mail. Really Noble, you should be ashamed of yourself, no class, too many red flags. I think you will always be alone and lonely because you don't have the balls to change. Ginny

The last thing I did in Minneapolis was put down a $400 deposit on a puppy that I would pick up in six weeks when I was scheduled to come back after the Tahoe reunion and my cousin Caitlyn's wedding in September. My friends Linda and Bill were the breeders, and after I saw their dog at Kimmie's party, I knew that was the breed I wanted. He was a five-week-old Tibetan terrier, more accurately a miniature sheepdog. He was the breed of the Dalai Lama. That sealed the deal. I fell in love the minute I saw him. There were a bunch of puppies in the litter, and he was the runt. They almost lost the whole litter because they all caught a virus. Linda and Bill had to stay up for forty-eight hours watching and administering medicine to keep them alive. Bill picked my puppy for me because he fought the hardest. Like me. I named him Photon after another dog I knew. It means a particle of light.

After connecting with many of my golden friends, I headed to Rapid City, South Dakota, to stay with my sorority sister Mary and her husband Greg. I drove another eight hours to their house, which was practically a stone's throw from Mt. Rushmore and Crazy Horse. I was blown away by the natural beauty always surrounding me on my road trip through America. I was feeling so patriotic and grateful for my magical life and so struck by the fact that one year ago I thought I was dying a long, slow, painful death. Mary and I reconnected after many years of not communicating at all and found that our friendship was just on a long hiatus. Being together was like no time had passed as often happens with those special friends in one's life. She drove me to see Mt. Rushmore and then the amazing head of Crazy Horse, which is a work in progress and most likely will never be finished. She saved her favorite tour for last. She called it the national park of the erect penises. It was true—a place of amazement where all the rock formations looked like that. It went on and on until we both laughed so hard and exclaimed at the magnificence of them. The night before I left on the final leg of my trip where I would drop down into Colorado and the Springs, we traveled back in time together—the time during the late sixties when I was a midwestern girl from Minneapolis engaged to a first lieutenant going off to war in Vietnam. It was a revolution—a giant transition from old to completely new: 1967, 1968, 1969—a reorganization of our lives. We loved that we grew up during that very special time. A complete political, moral, ethical, musical, and *sexual* revolution. Right on, right on.

I was so ready to get on the road in the morning. I missed my grandchildren and Page. I missed all my girlfriends. I missed Matt and Ara and Nikki and Gus. I followed Mary and Greg out of the driveway of their awesome house in the Black Hills of South Dakota. They made sure I made it to the junction of I-25 where I would have a straight shot south into the Springs through Ft. Collins and Denver. It was a piece of cake except for the speeding ticket I got in Wyoming. Apparently I was going eighty in a sixty-five. They don't post the speed limit signs in Wyoming for hundreds of miles. The cop said I should have studied up. He was an asshole. I was fascinated by all the hundreds of Harleys riding in a steady stream heading up to Sturgis for the weekend. I had met a couple of gorgeous girls riding tandem on a totally tricked out custom cherry red Harley when I stopped for gas. They had full leathers on and were sexy girls whether they were lovers or friends. I told them I was a breast cancer survivor during our conversation. They came over to my car and high-fived me. It's easy to bond with women. After the ticket I put my car on cruise control and relaxed with my thoughts and music. The time flew by as I was getting closer and closer to the Springs. I was marveling at my beautiful life and feeling gratitude. I exited I-25 at Filmore and was feeling butterflies in my stomach as I turned left on Mesa only blocks from my house. It had been gently raining for the last hour or so. I looked to my left and a magnificent full spectrum rainbow appeared in the big open field. I pulled over to the side of the road, pulled my camera out of my purse, and with a click, click five times, caught the entire arch. I put the camera back in my purse and looked back for another glimpse; it was gone. I had the proof in my camera in case no one believed me. Was the universe smiling at me? I think so. I think it was saying, "Good job, Ginny! Keep on smiling. Be happy!"

It is the beginning, is it not?

My grandkids, Page and Photon

Taylor and Griffin

Afterword

Writing these memoirs has been a bit like riding a bike across the landscape of my life and observing from a distance how magical the ups and downs have really been. Most of the tragedies turned out to be miracles when I look through the lens of perspective.

I wrote Noble seven e-mails when I returned home from China, and he never answered one. I suppose I could find out where he is, but I don't really need to. He was the vehicle that got me to Dr. Li. I will always hold him in my heart for that.

Michael and I still share our daughter, Page, and Taylor and Griffin with much joy and happiness. I have twelve symbols in my life, which I have chosen to be like the twelve spokes of the Chinese Life Wheel. My symbols are the following:

Helen-Unconditional Love
Michael-Miracle Man
Page-Miracle Girl
Mark-Unconditional Friend
Sybil-Soul Mate
Dewayne-Generosity
Taylor-The Reward
Griffin-The Reward
Noble-The Vehicle
Dr. Li-The Healer
China-The Dream
Ginny-Happiness Heals

I'm sure there will be dozens more before my life is over. I have always felt life is a giant adventure, and I'm lucky and grateful to be on the ride of my lifetime. In my wildest imagination I could never have made up the story of what happened in my life. What a stupendous miracle I have lived. Thank the universe!